Jumbo Fashion

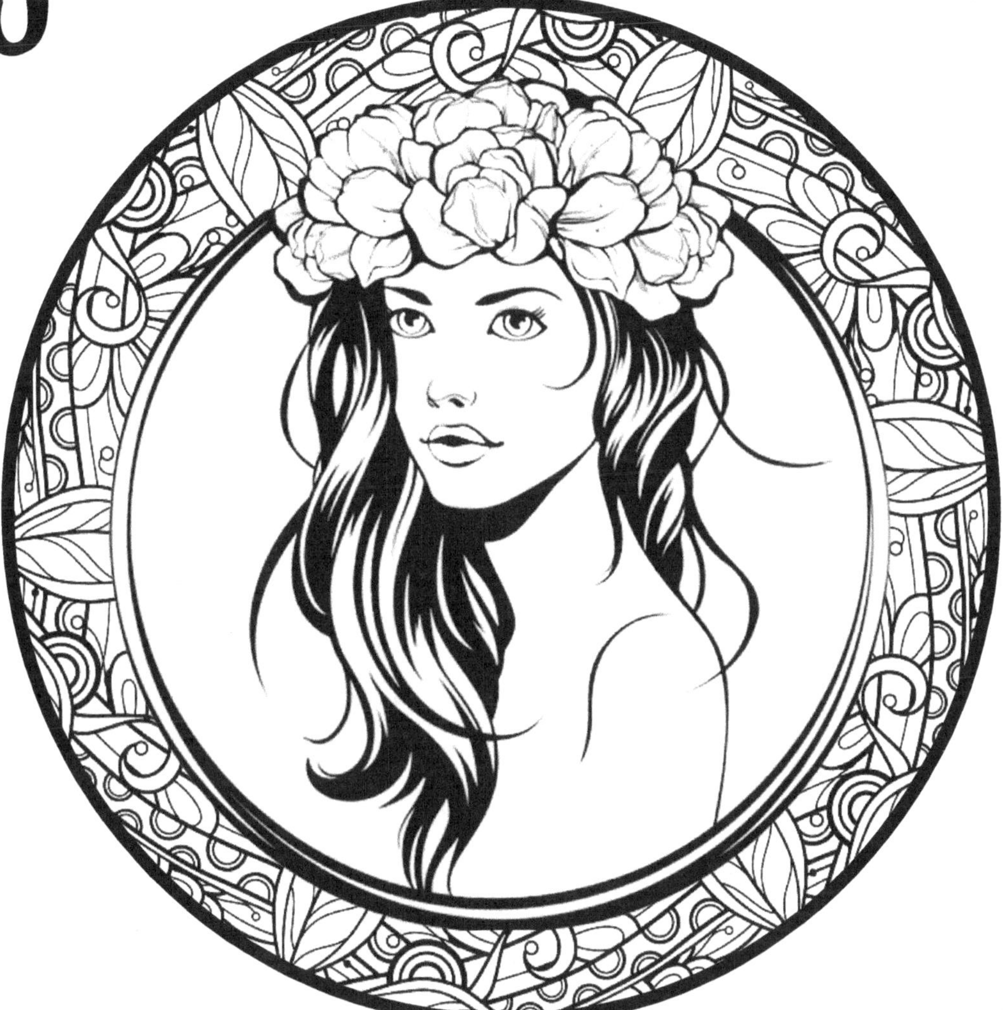

COLORING BOOK

FOR GIRLS

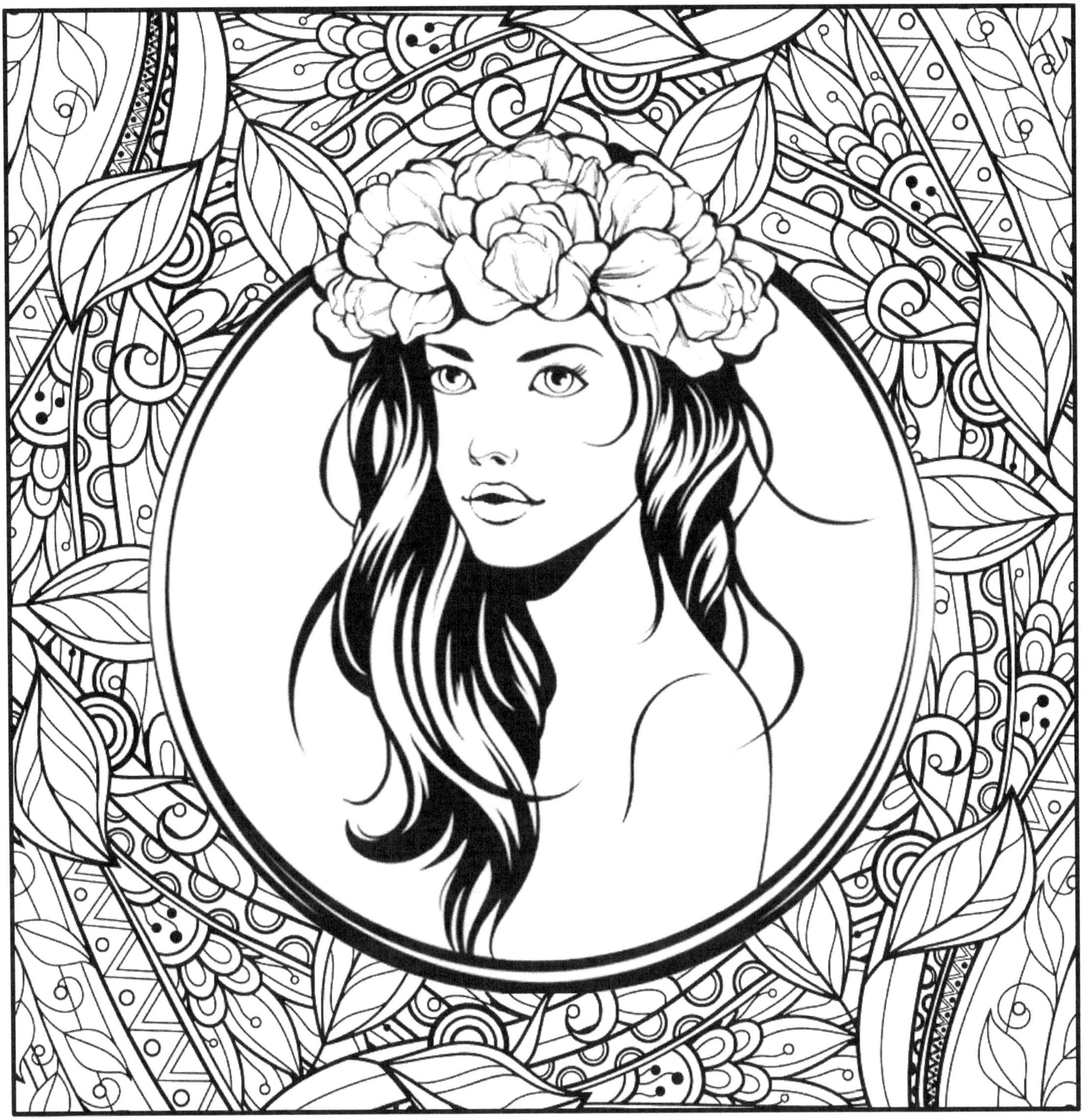

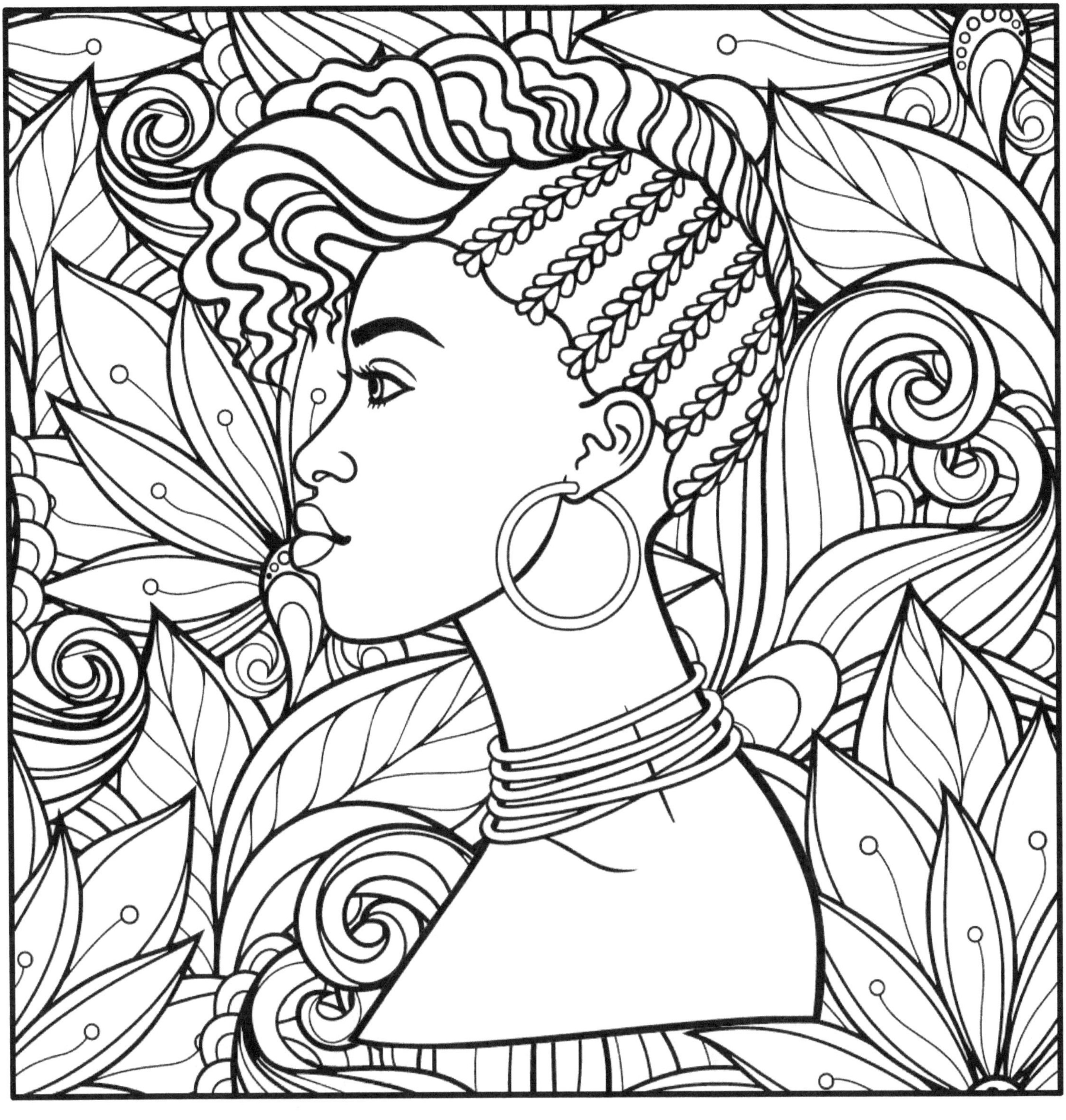

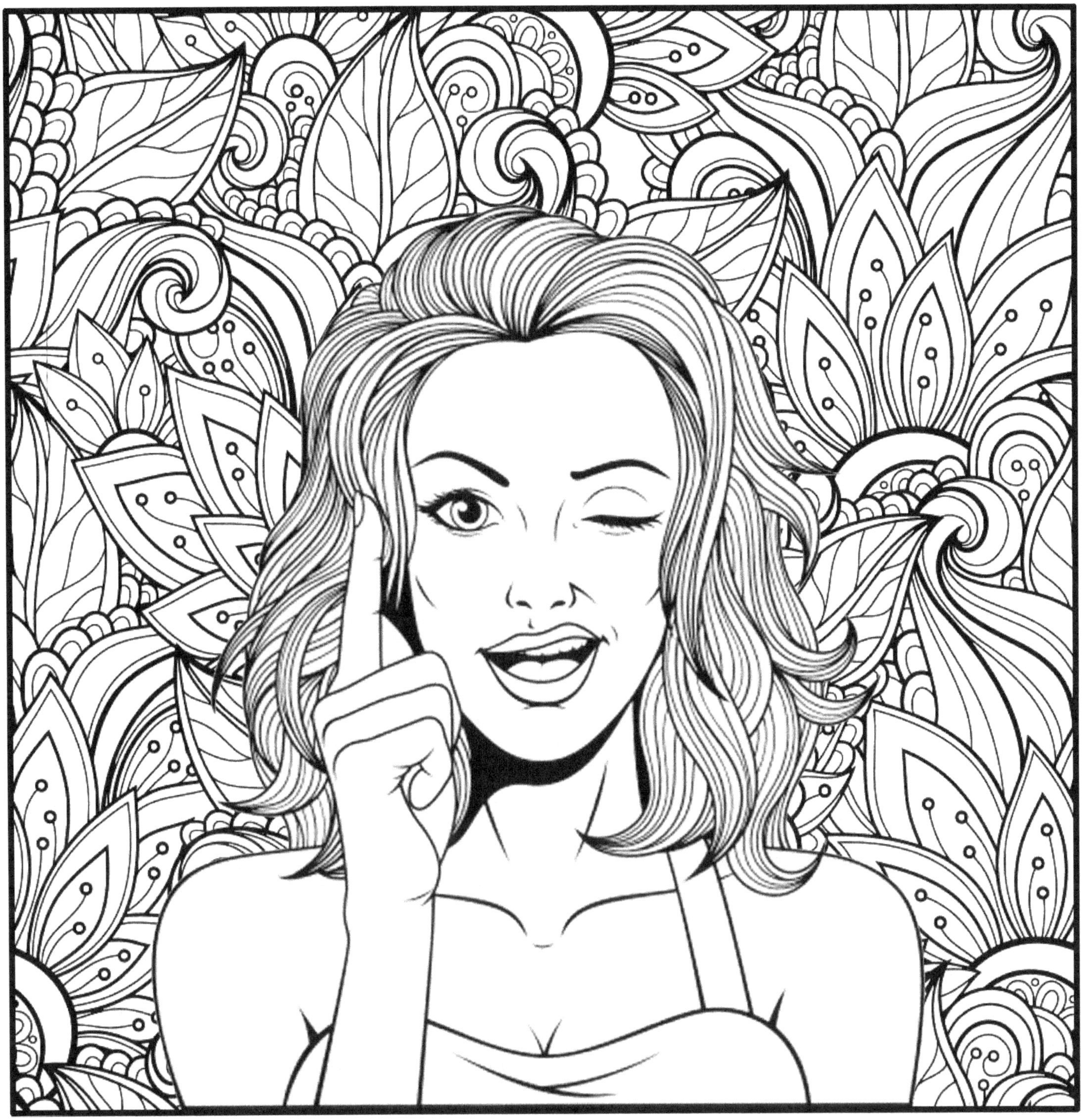

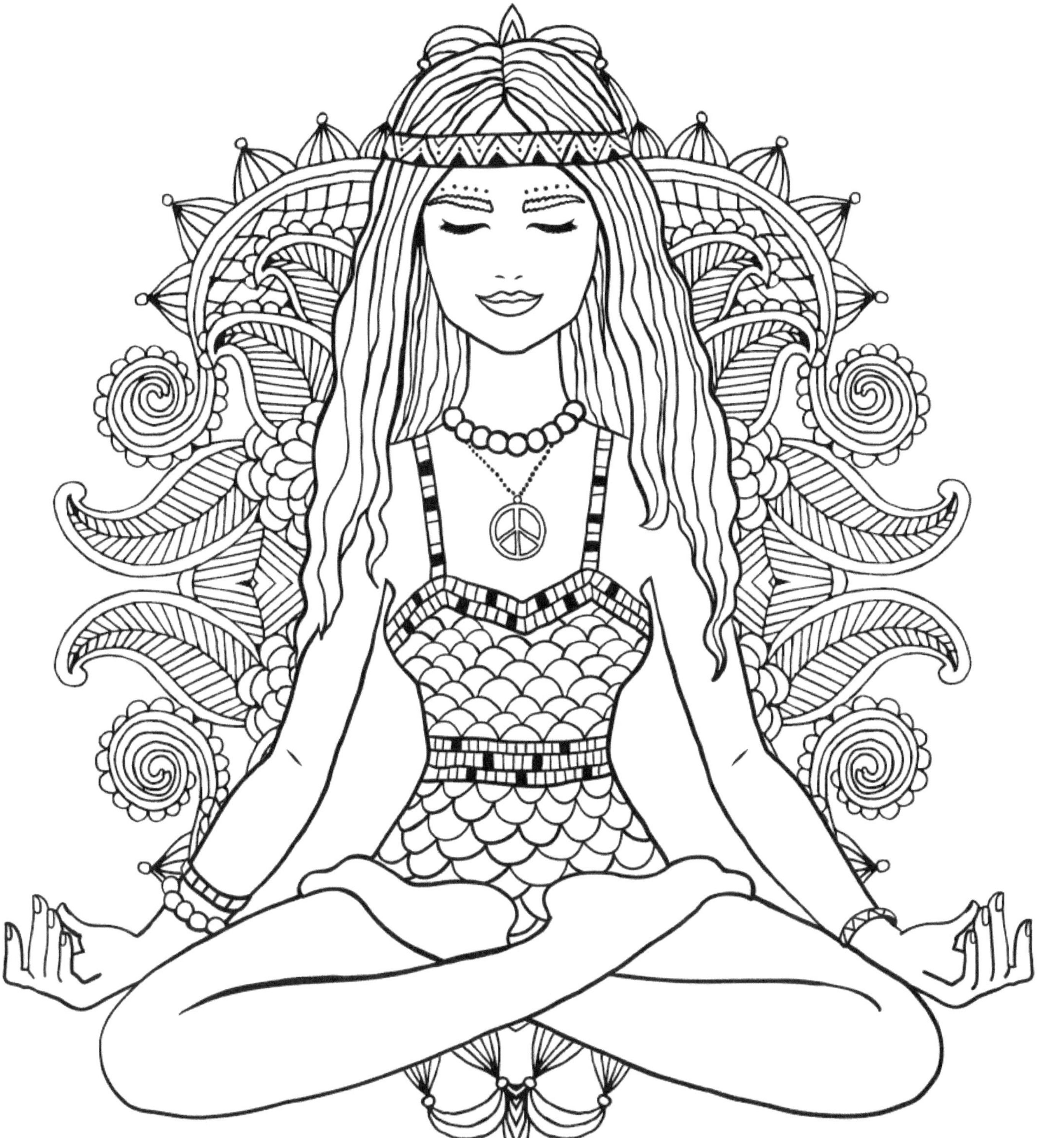

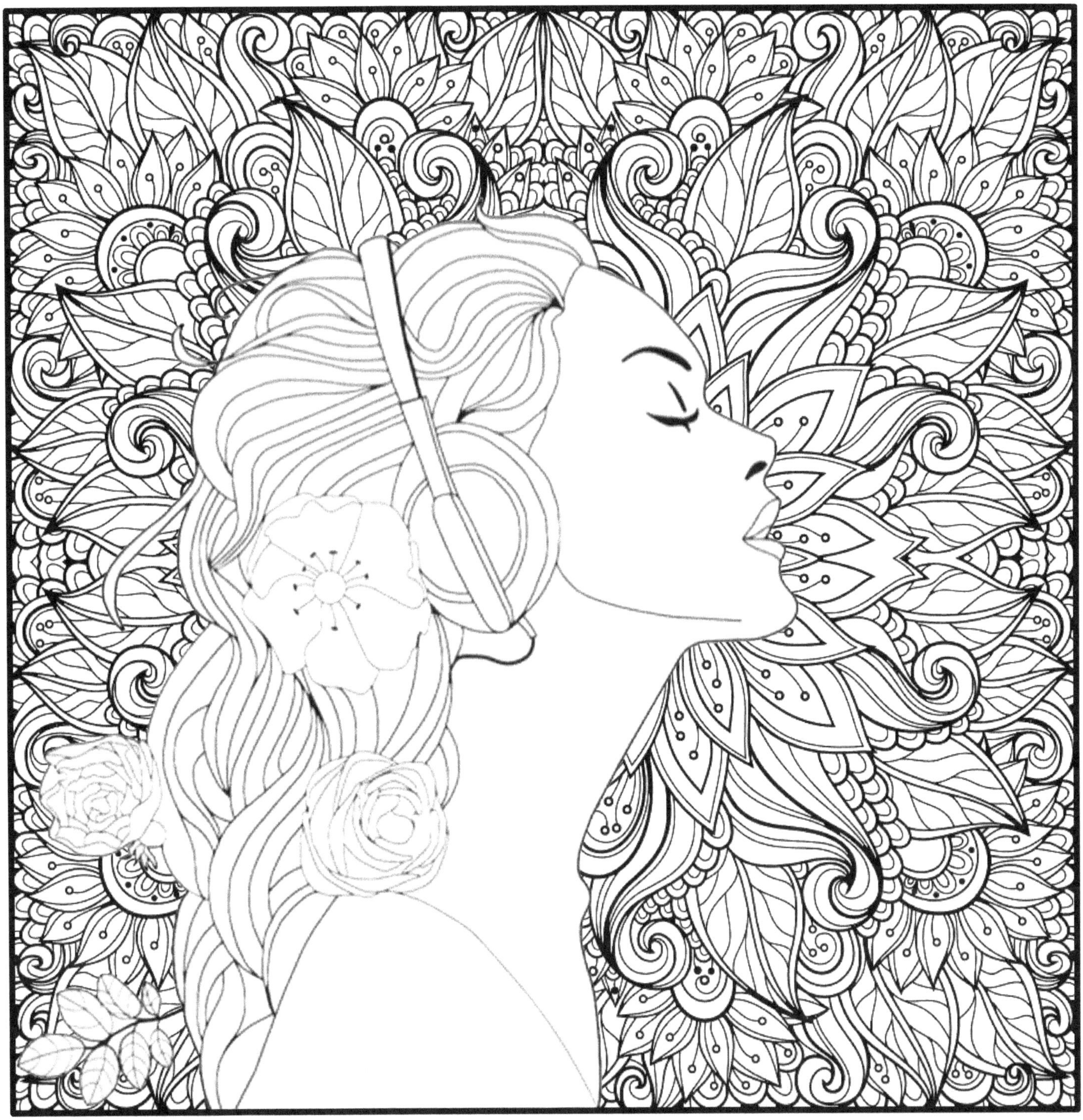

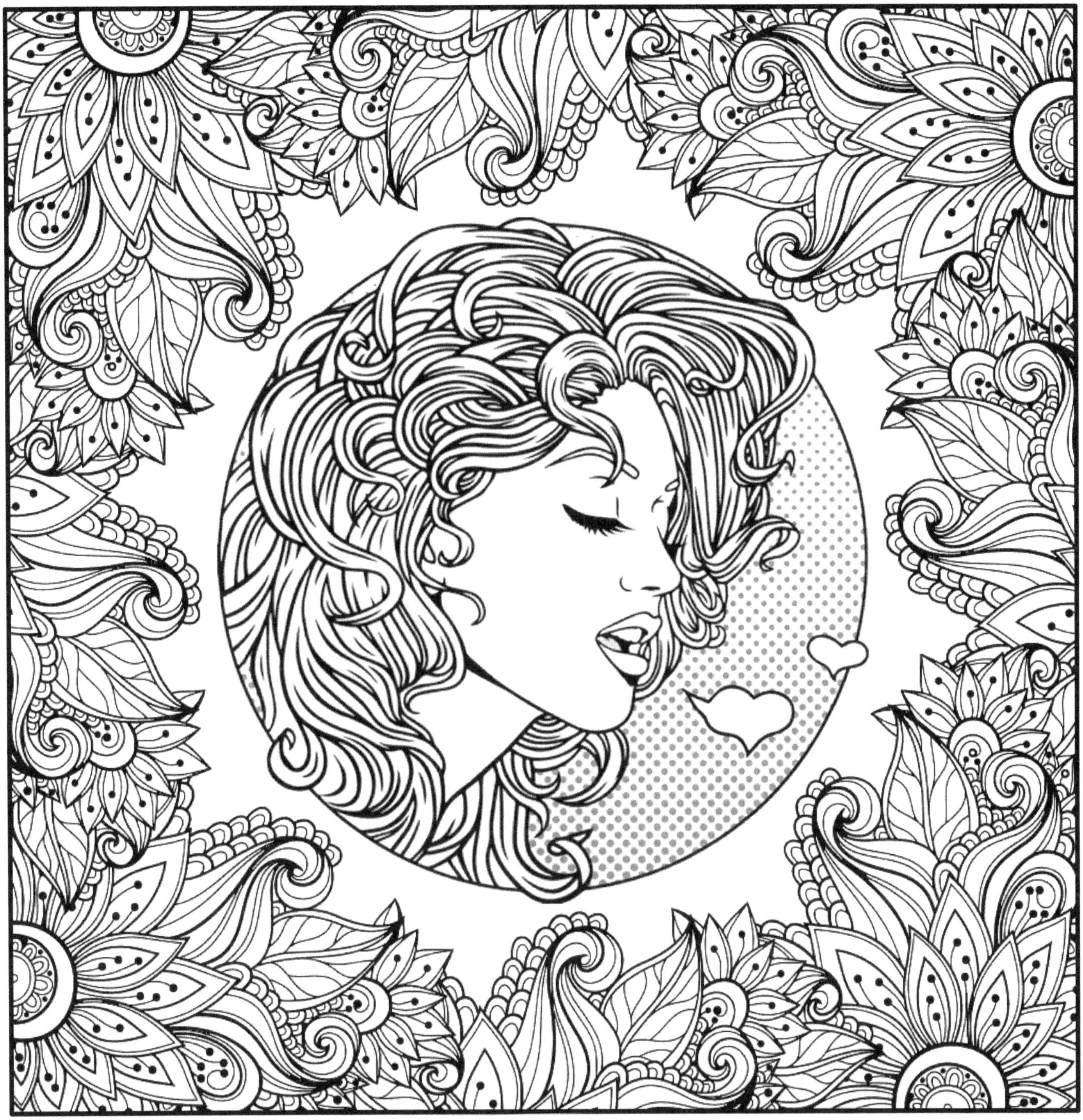

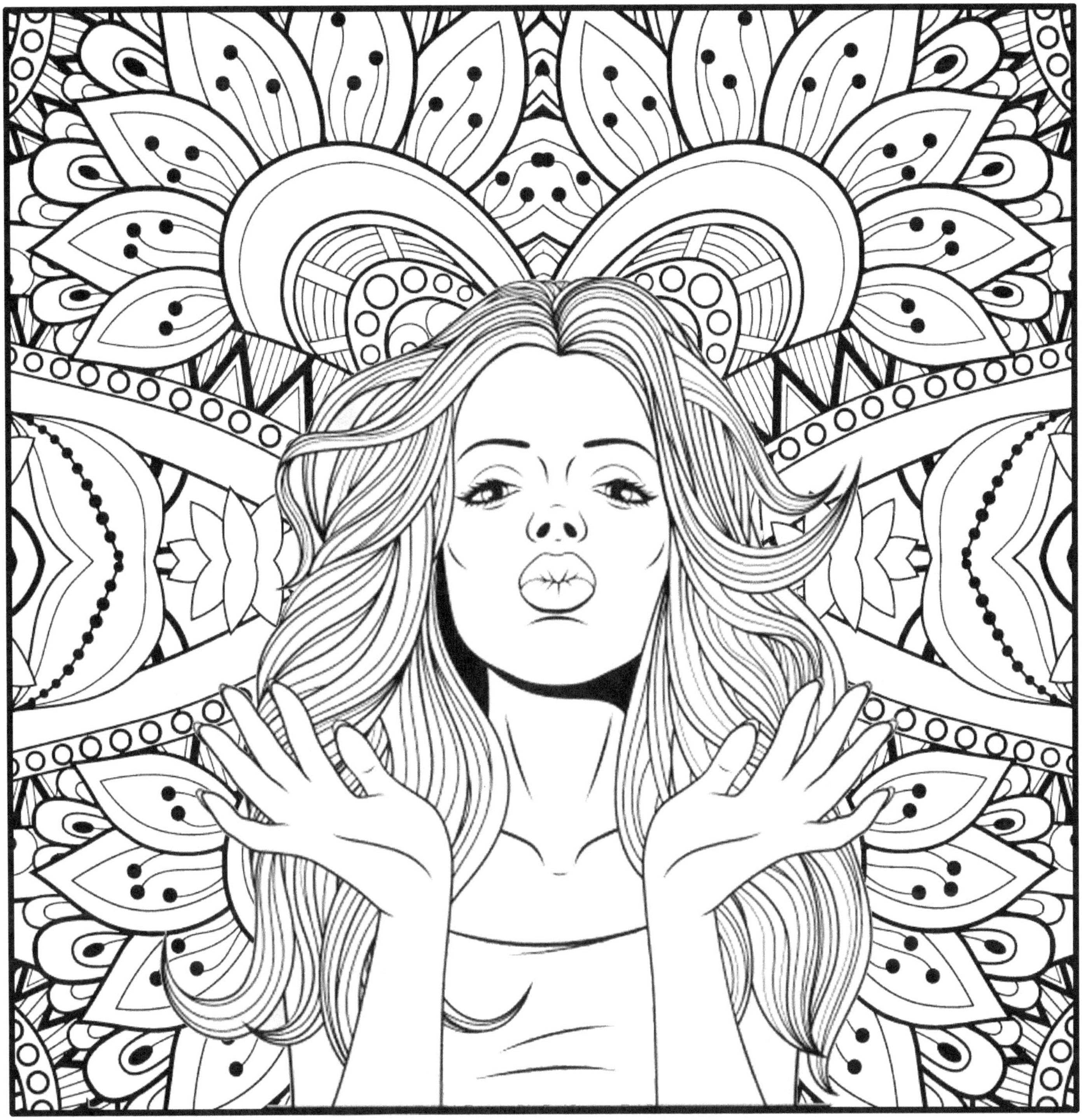

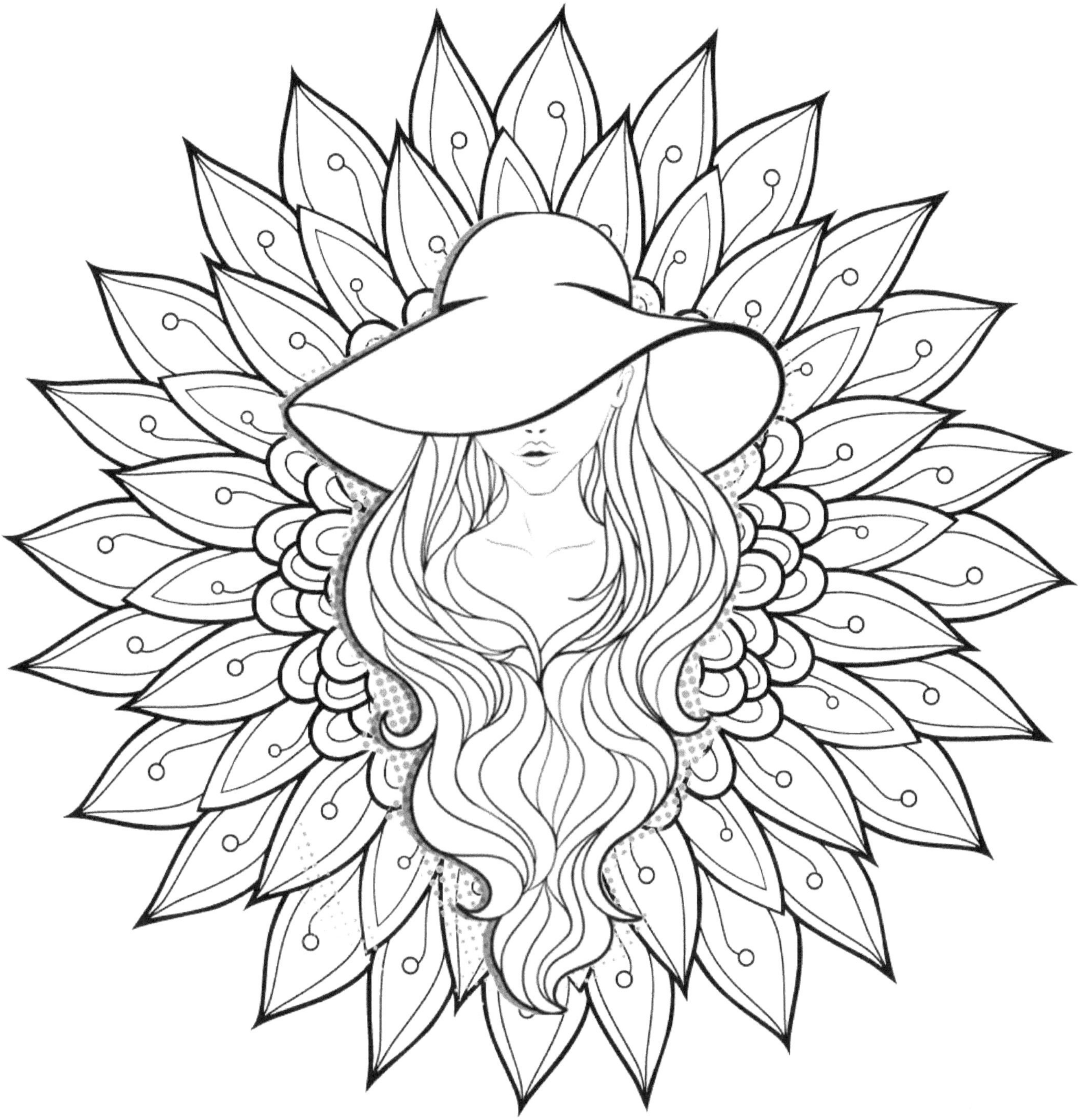

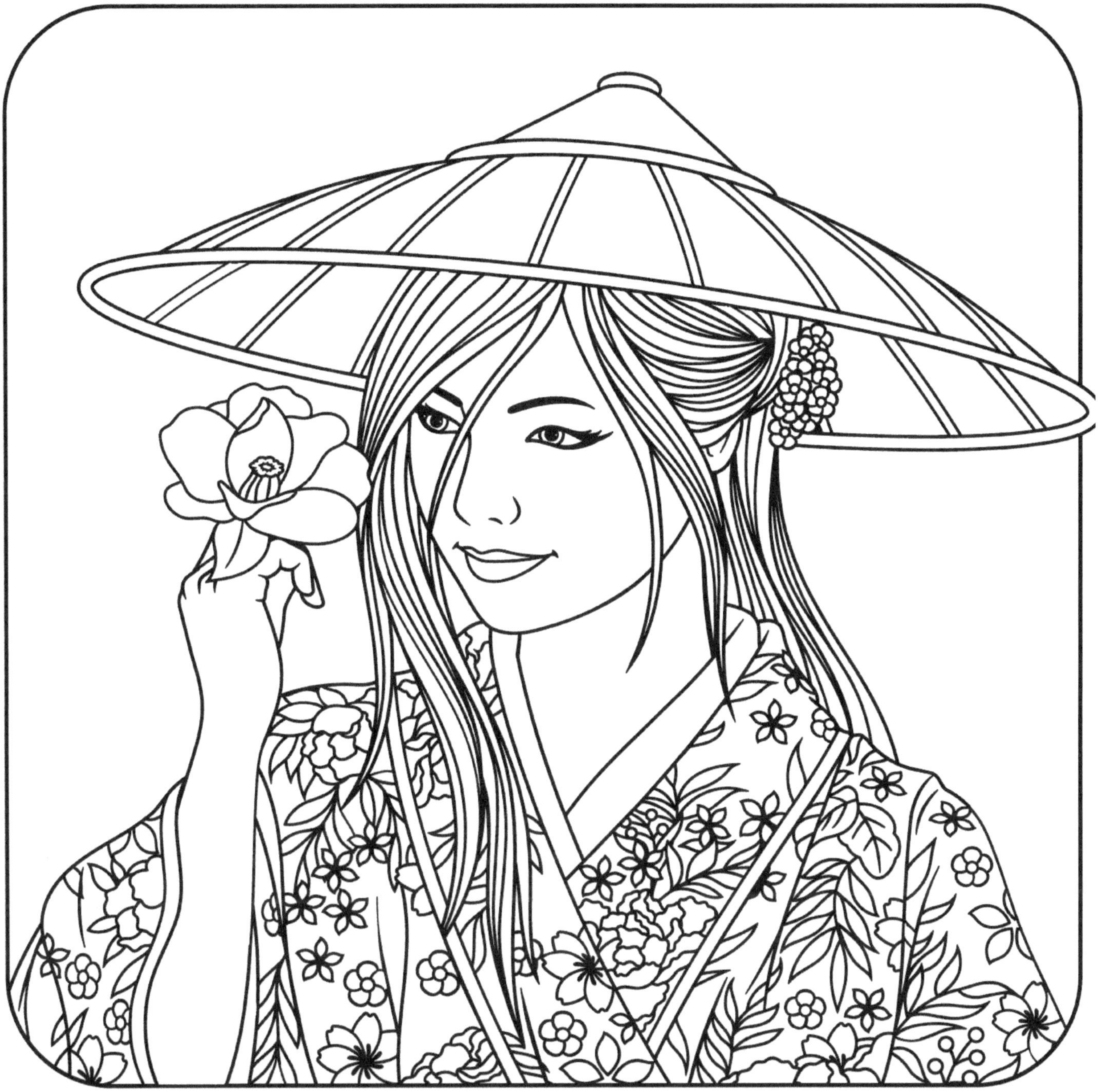

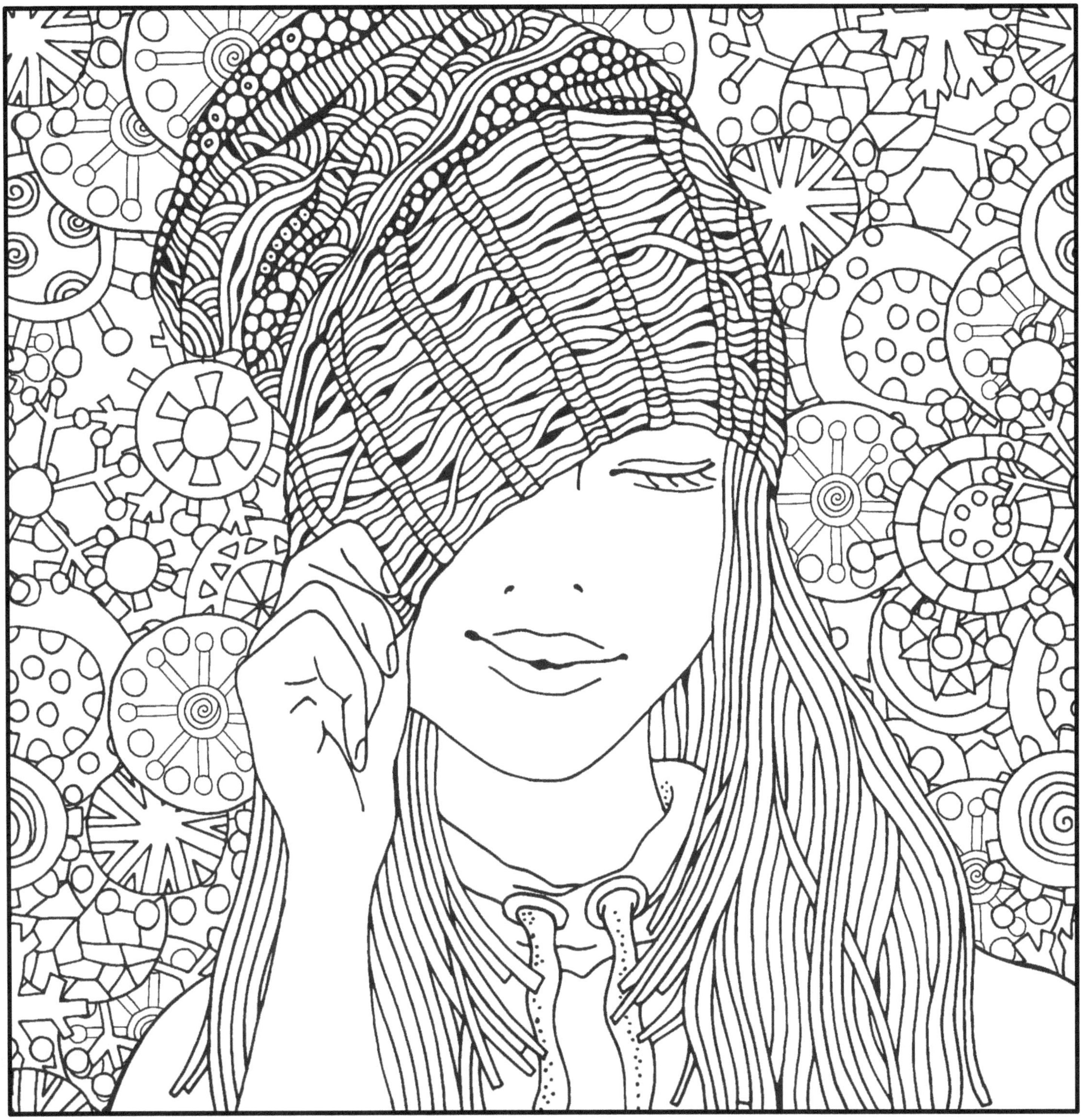

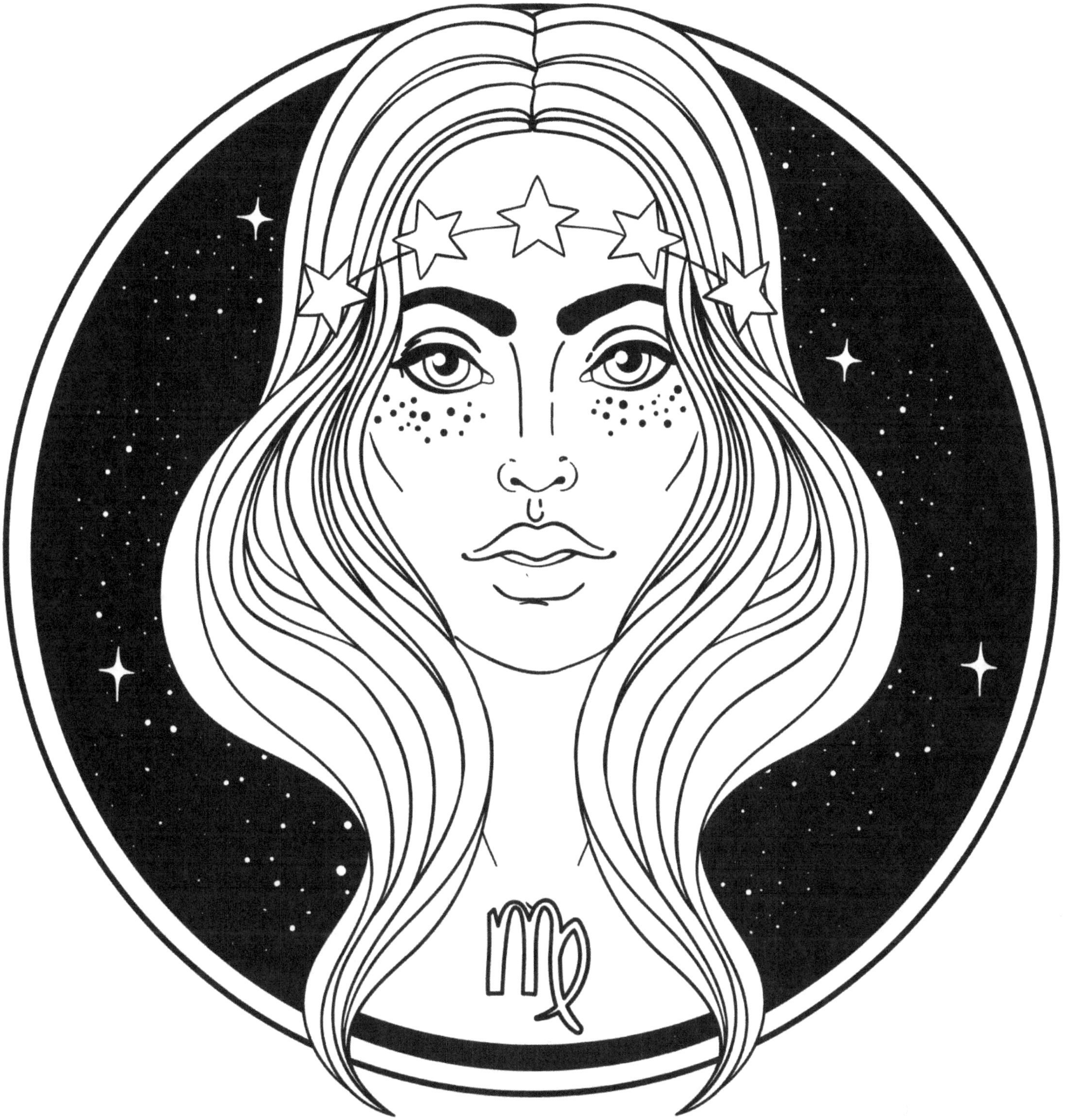

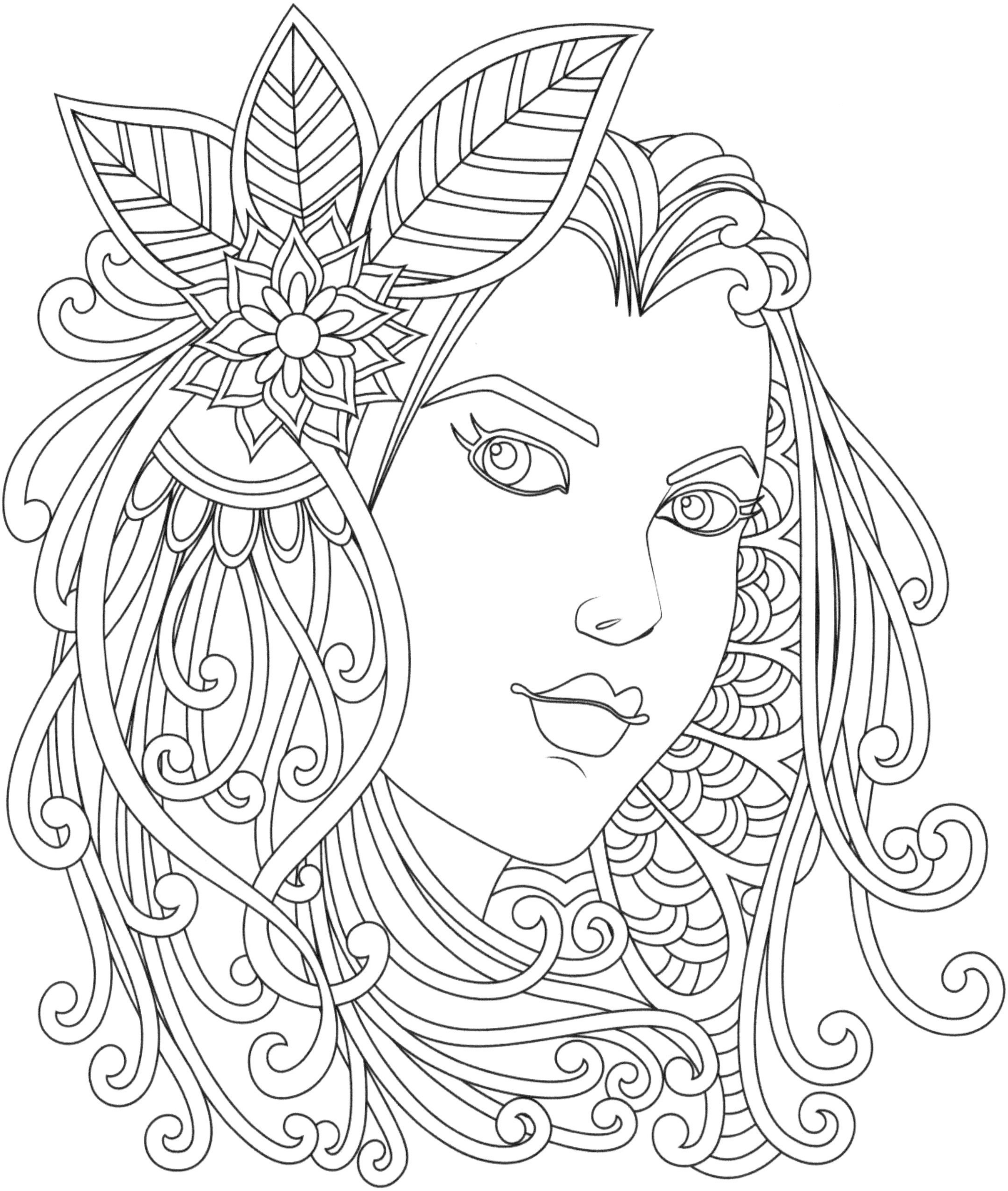

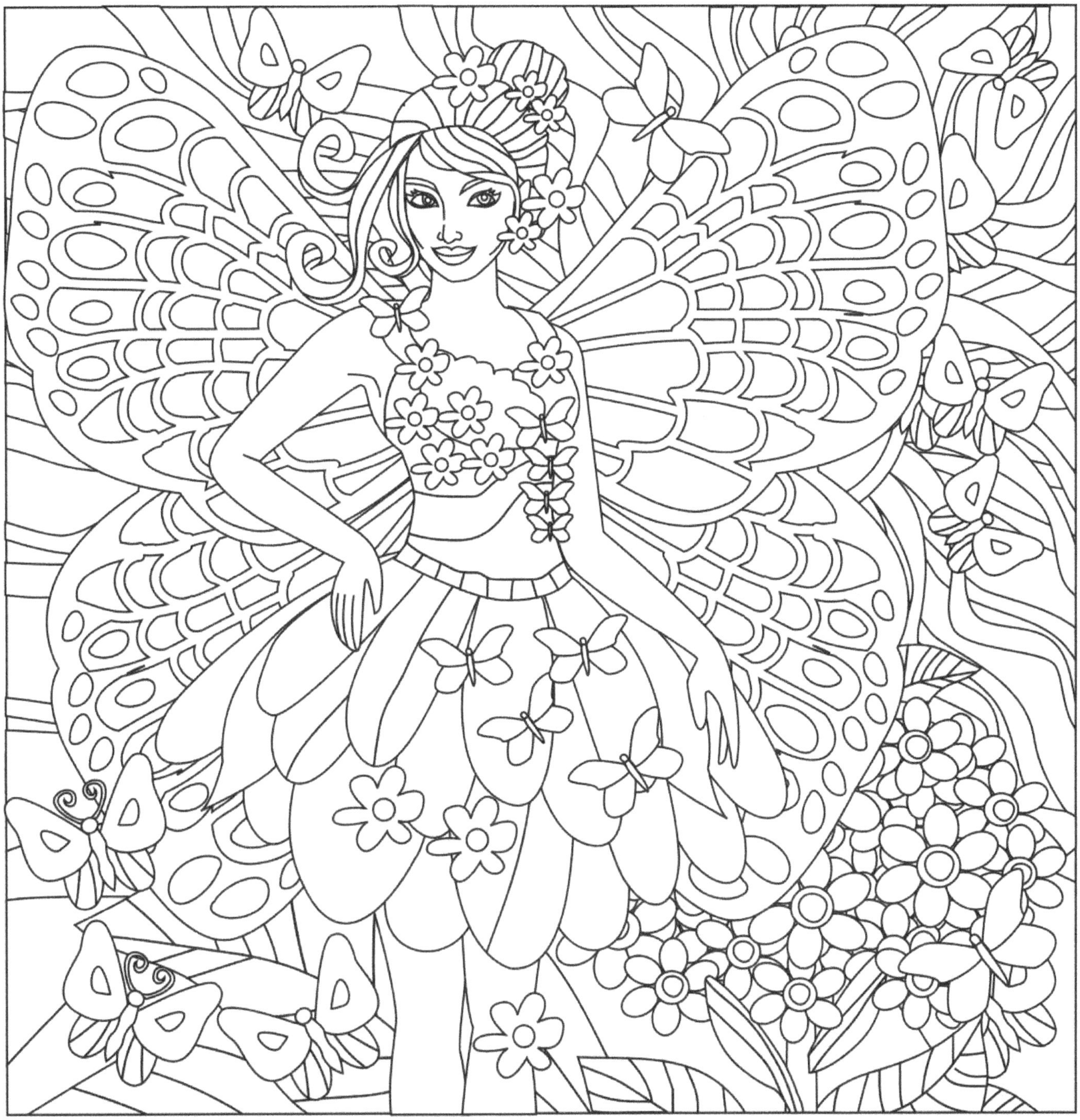

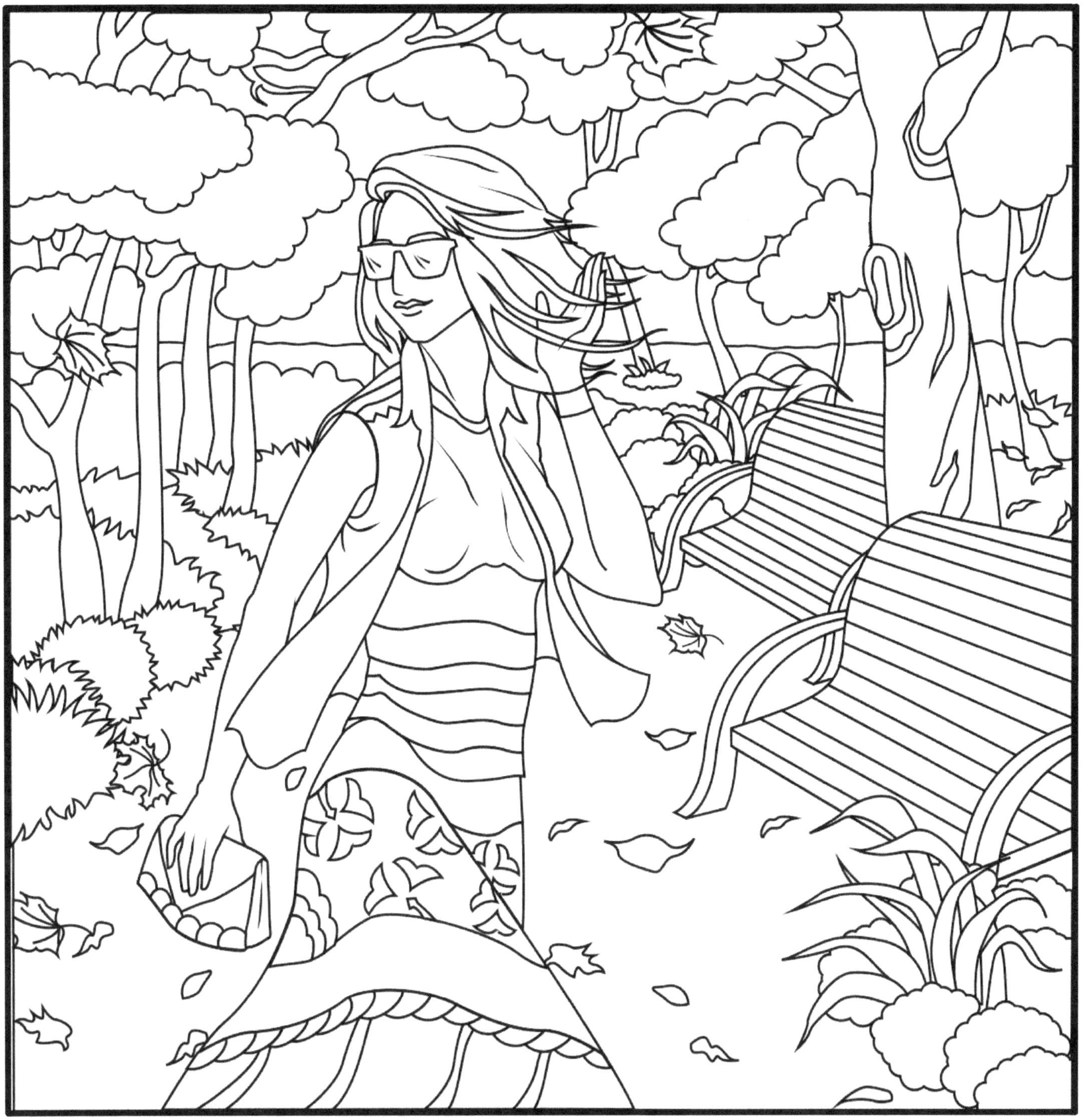

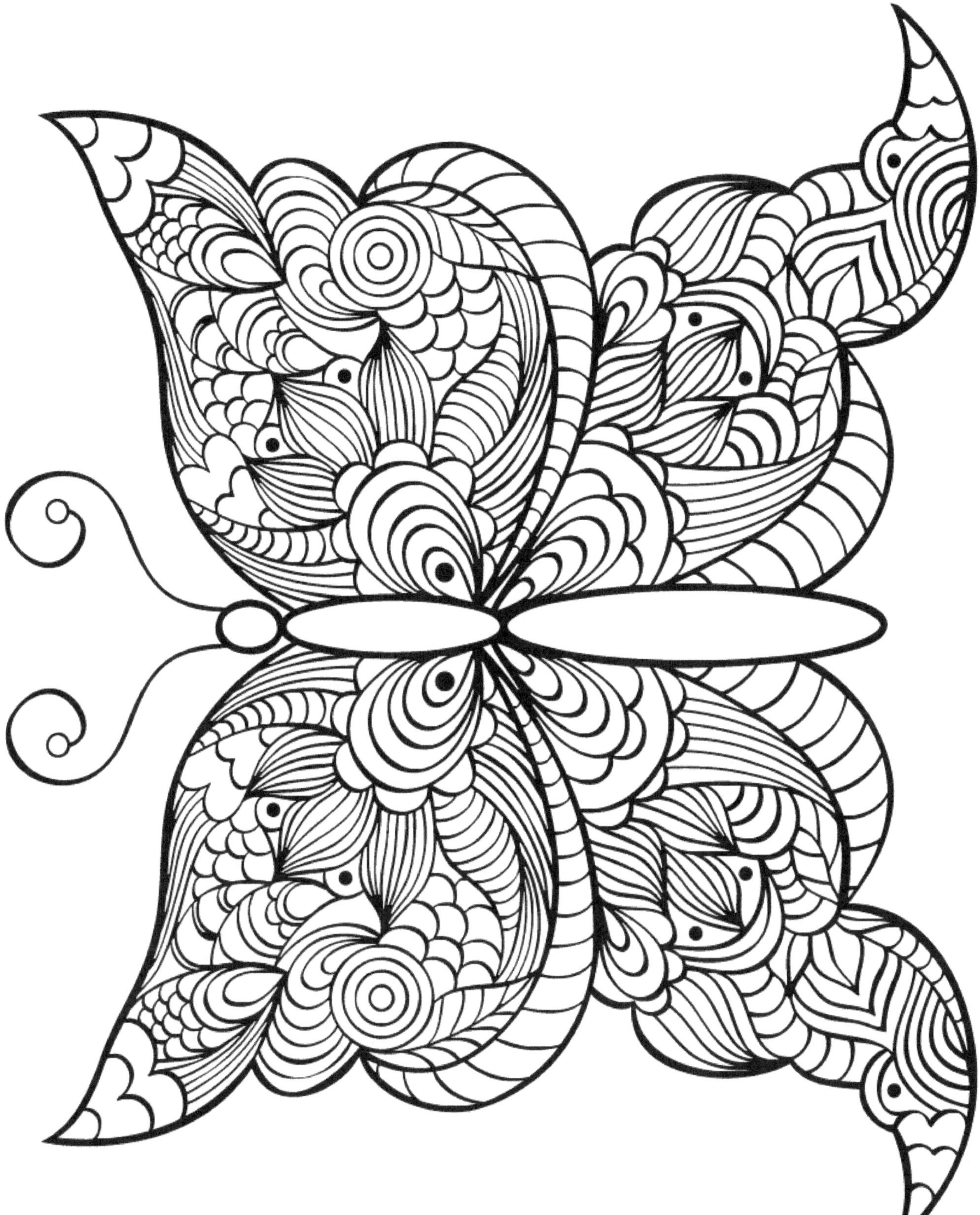

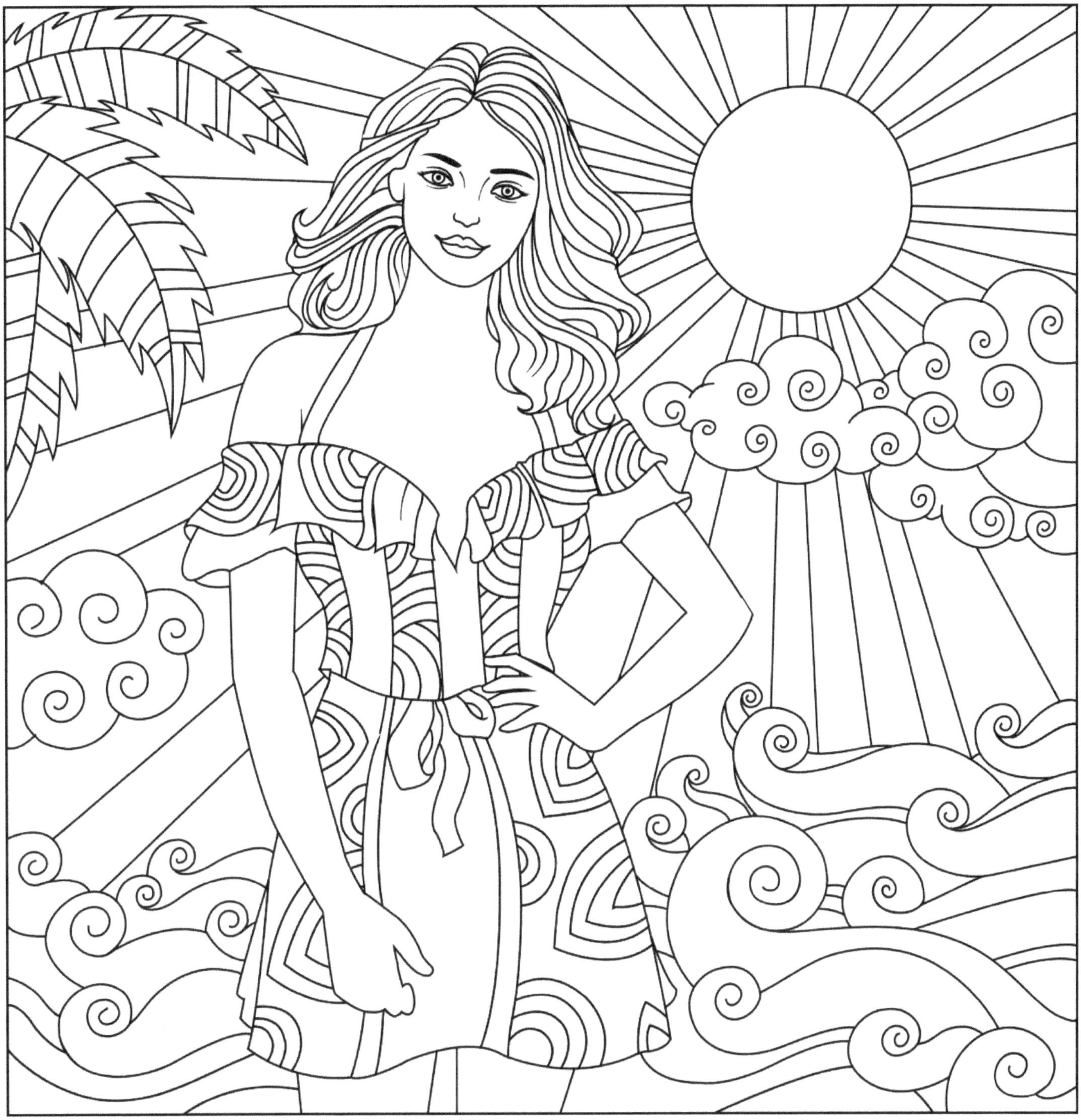

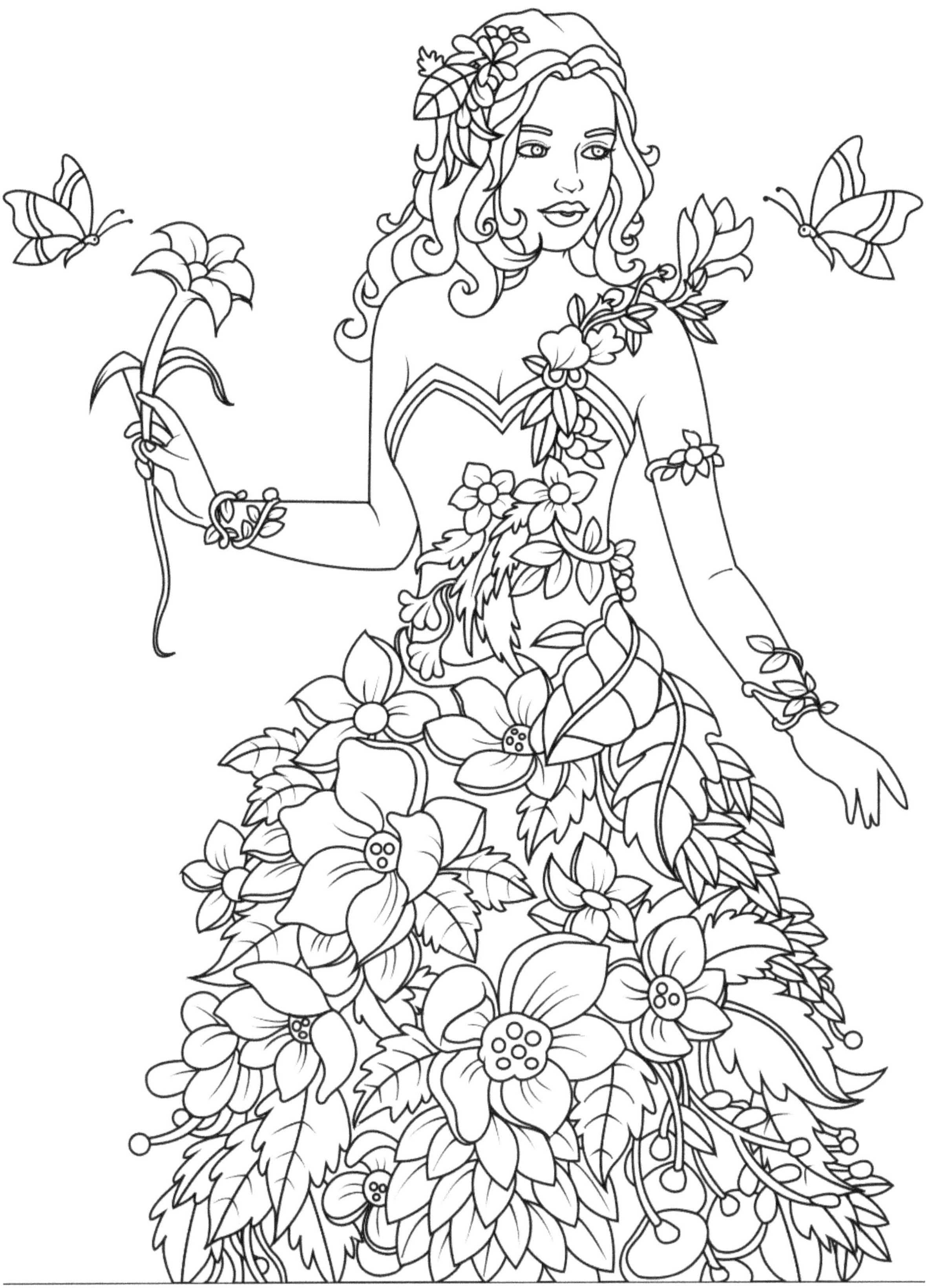

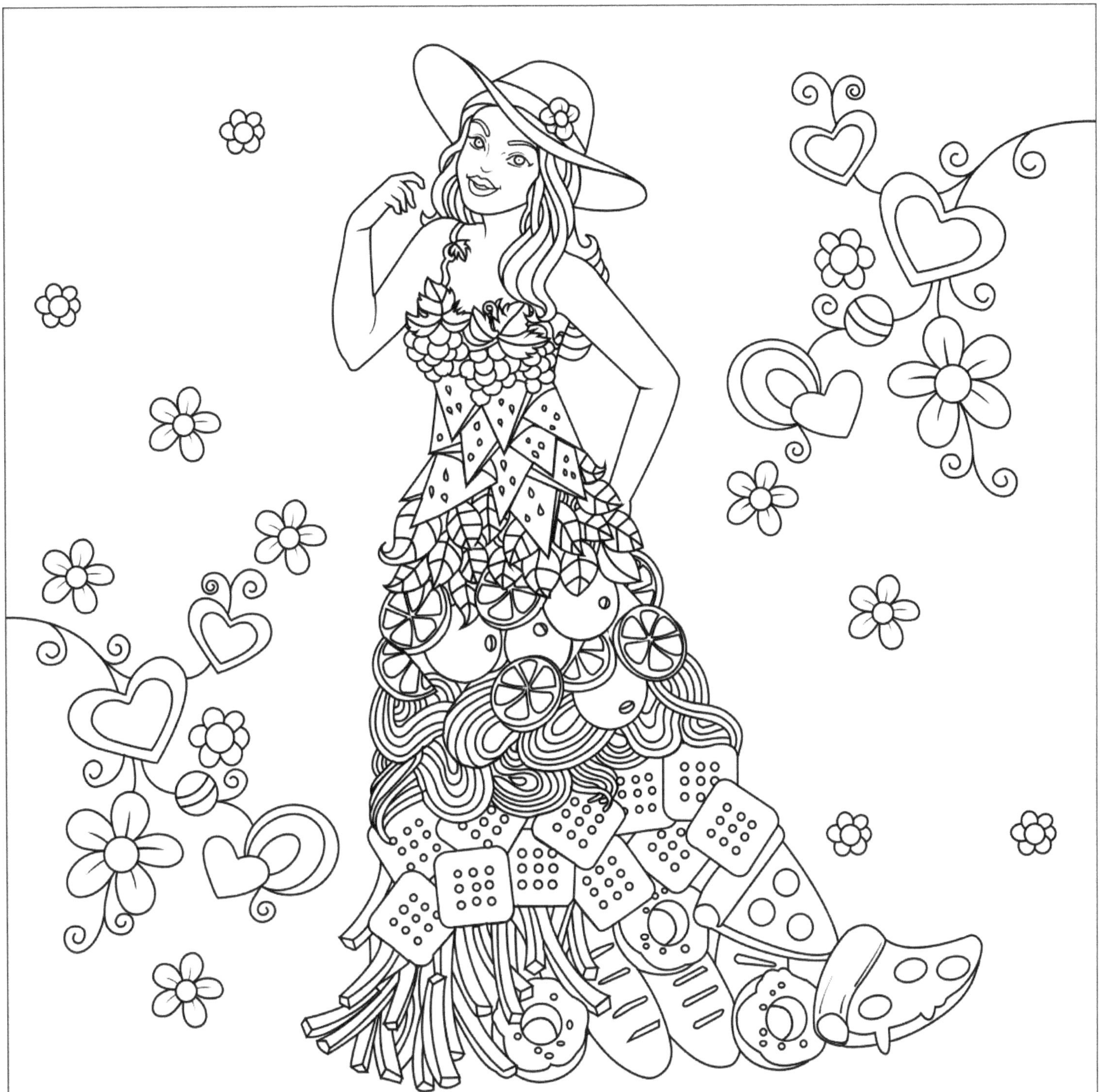

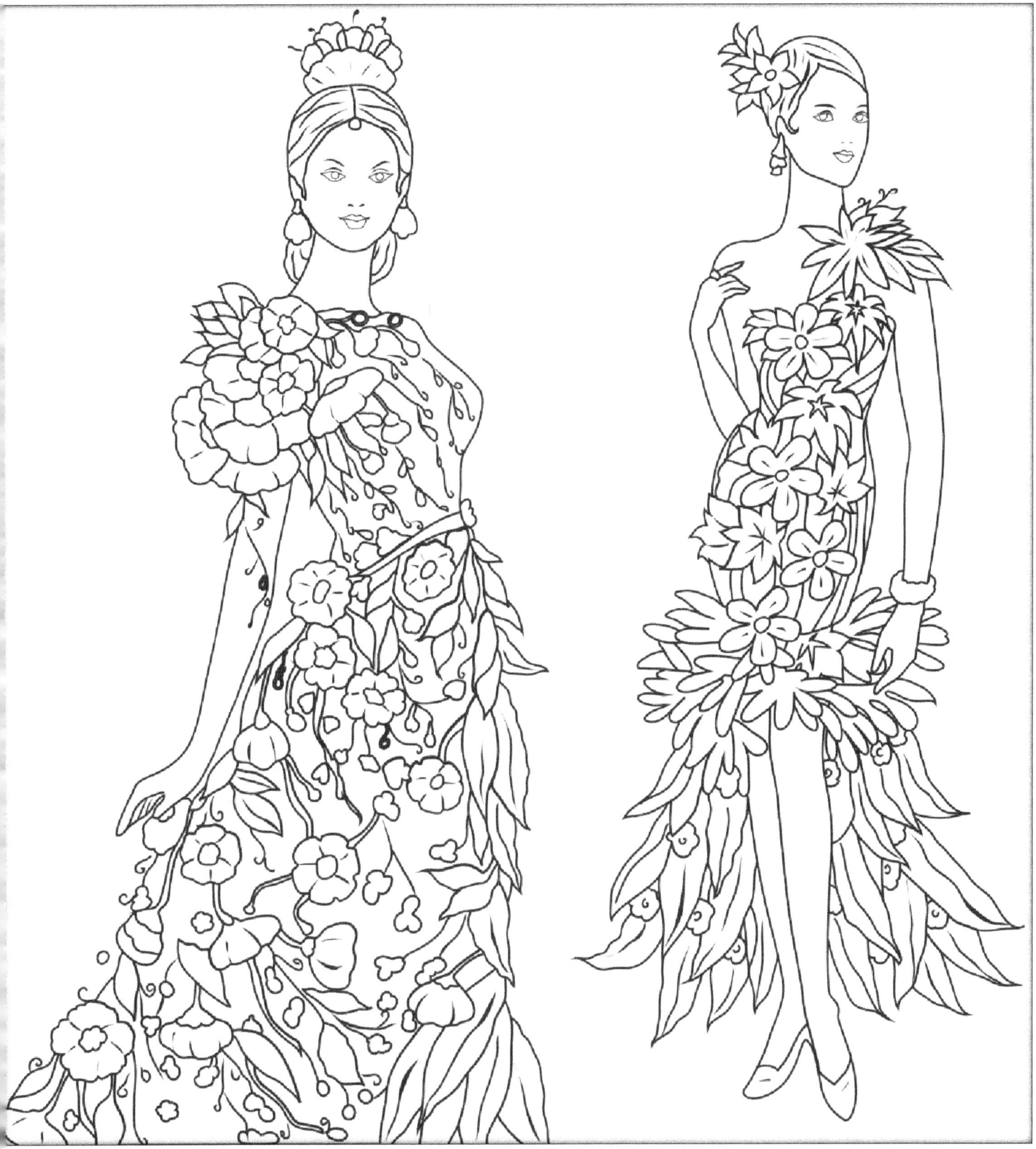

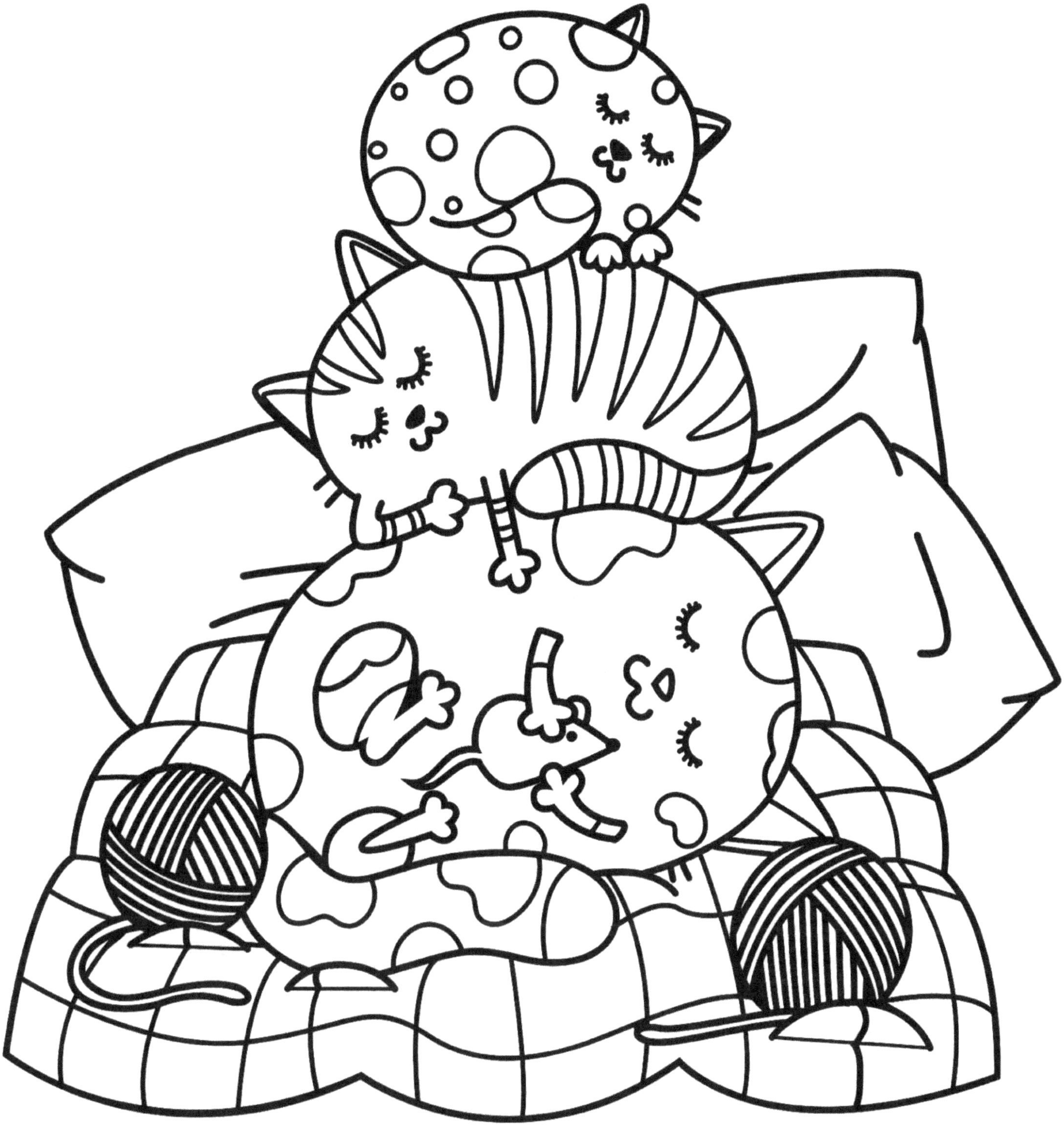

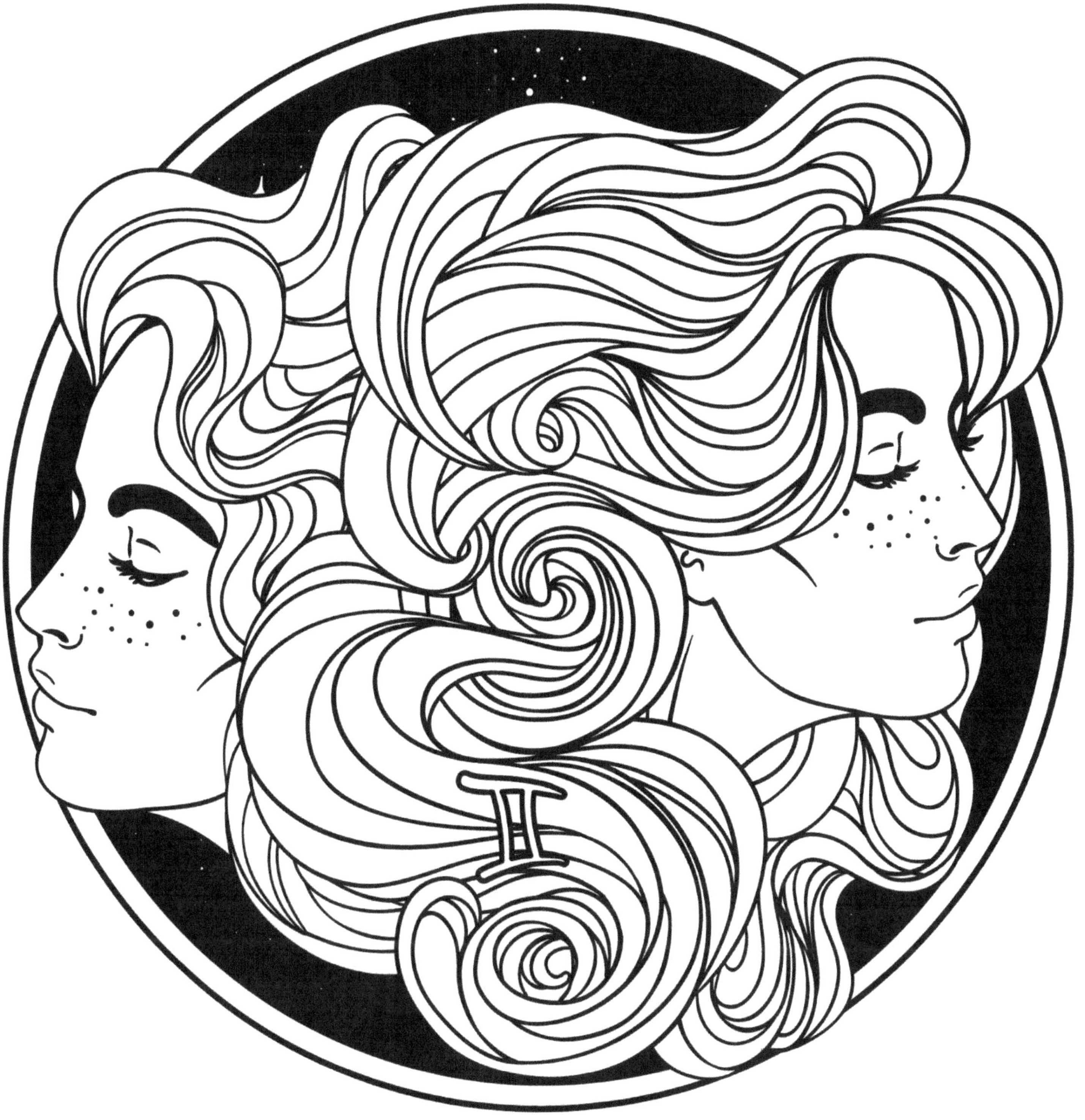

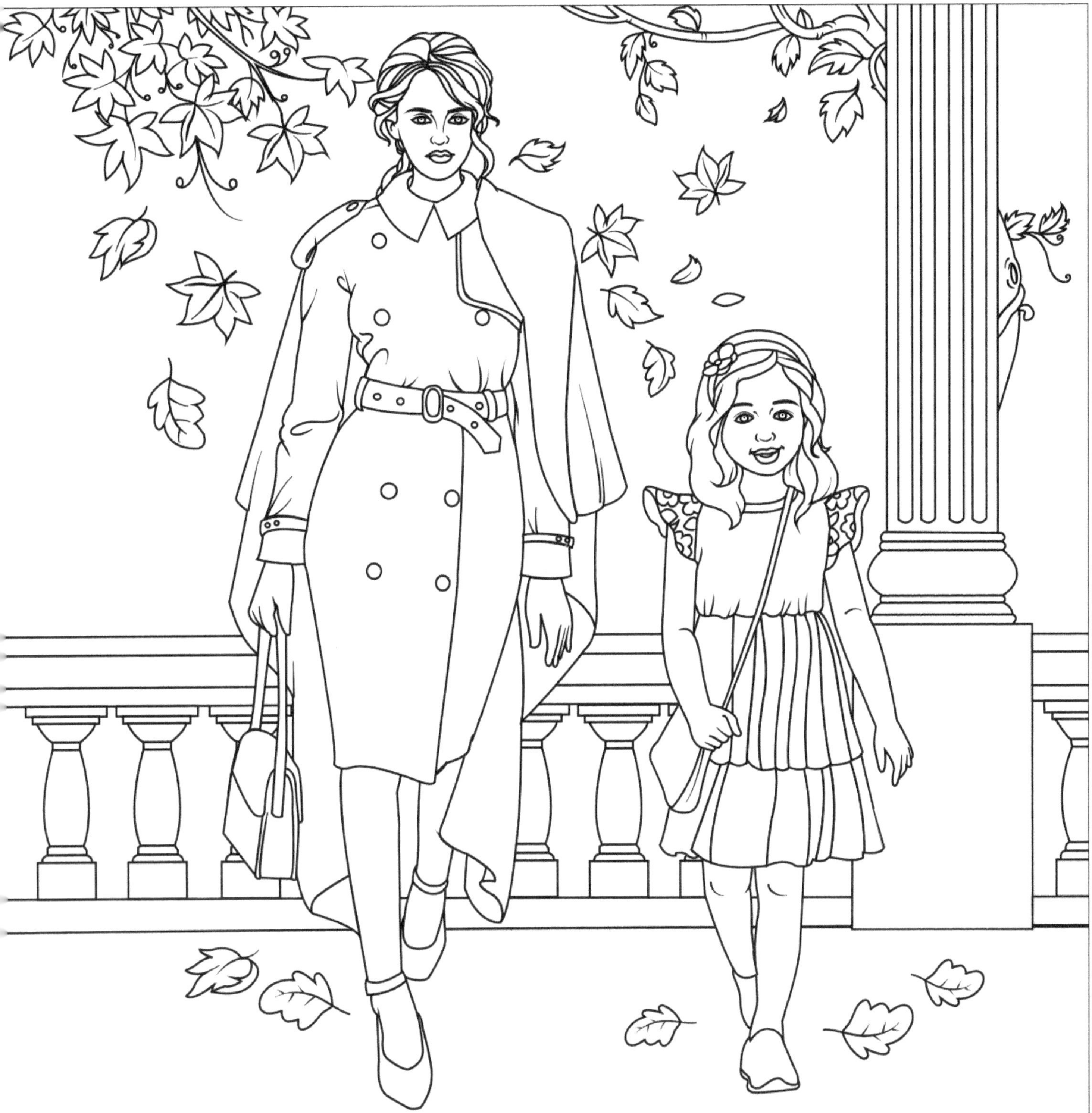

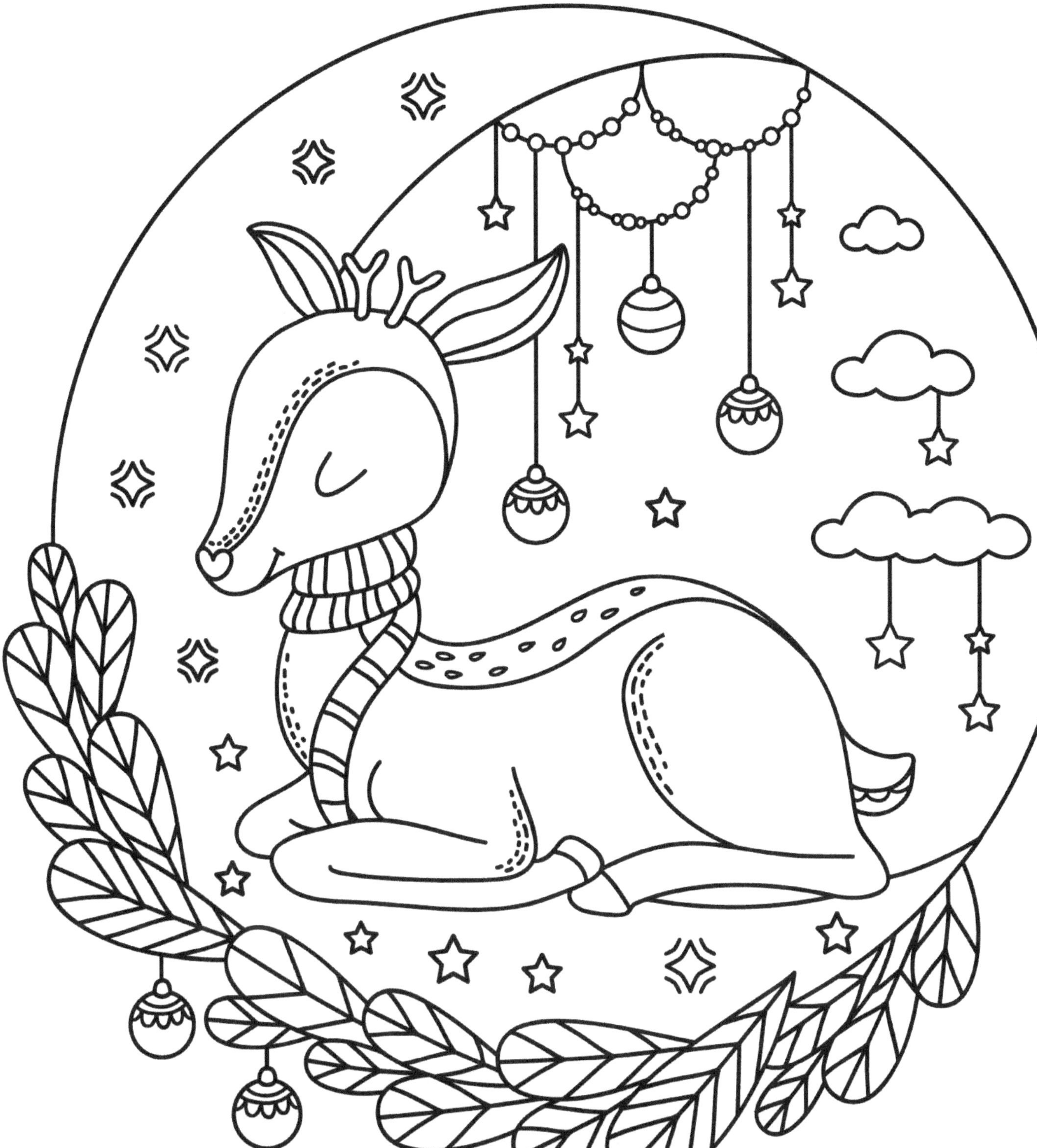

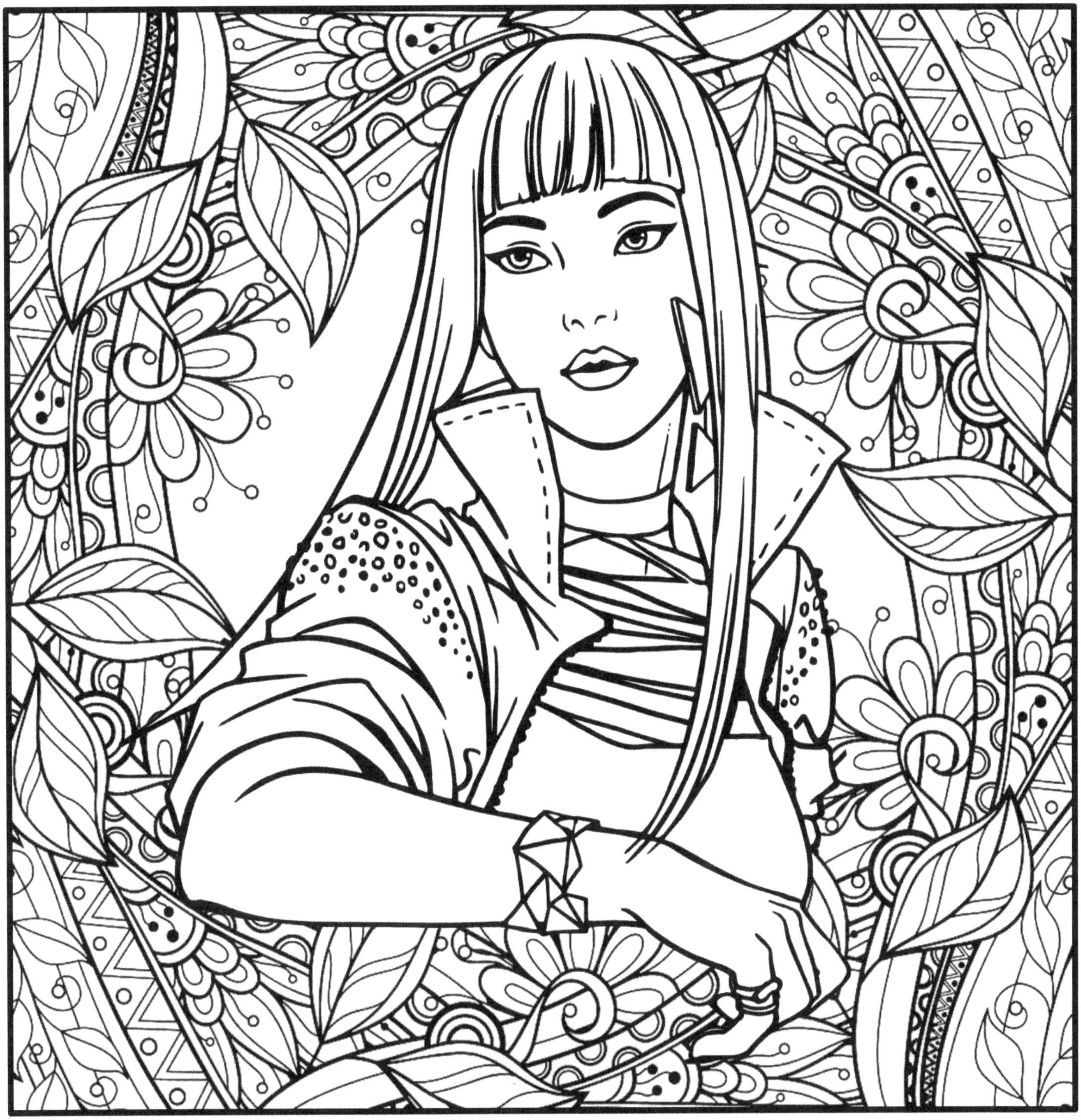

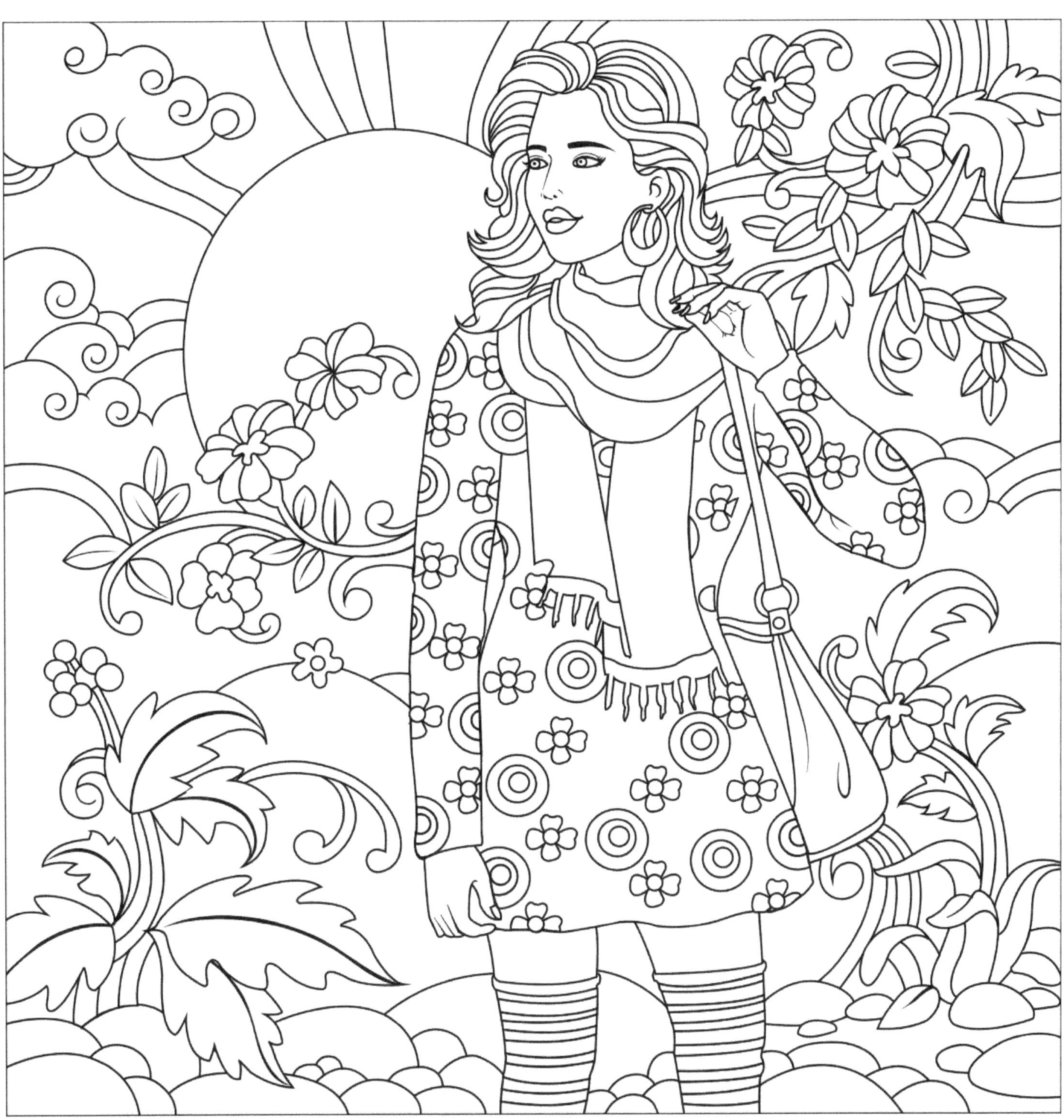

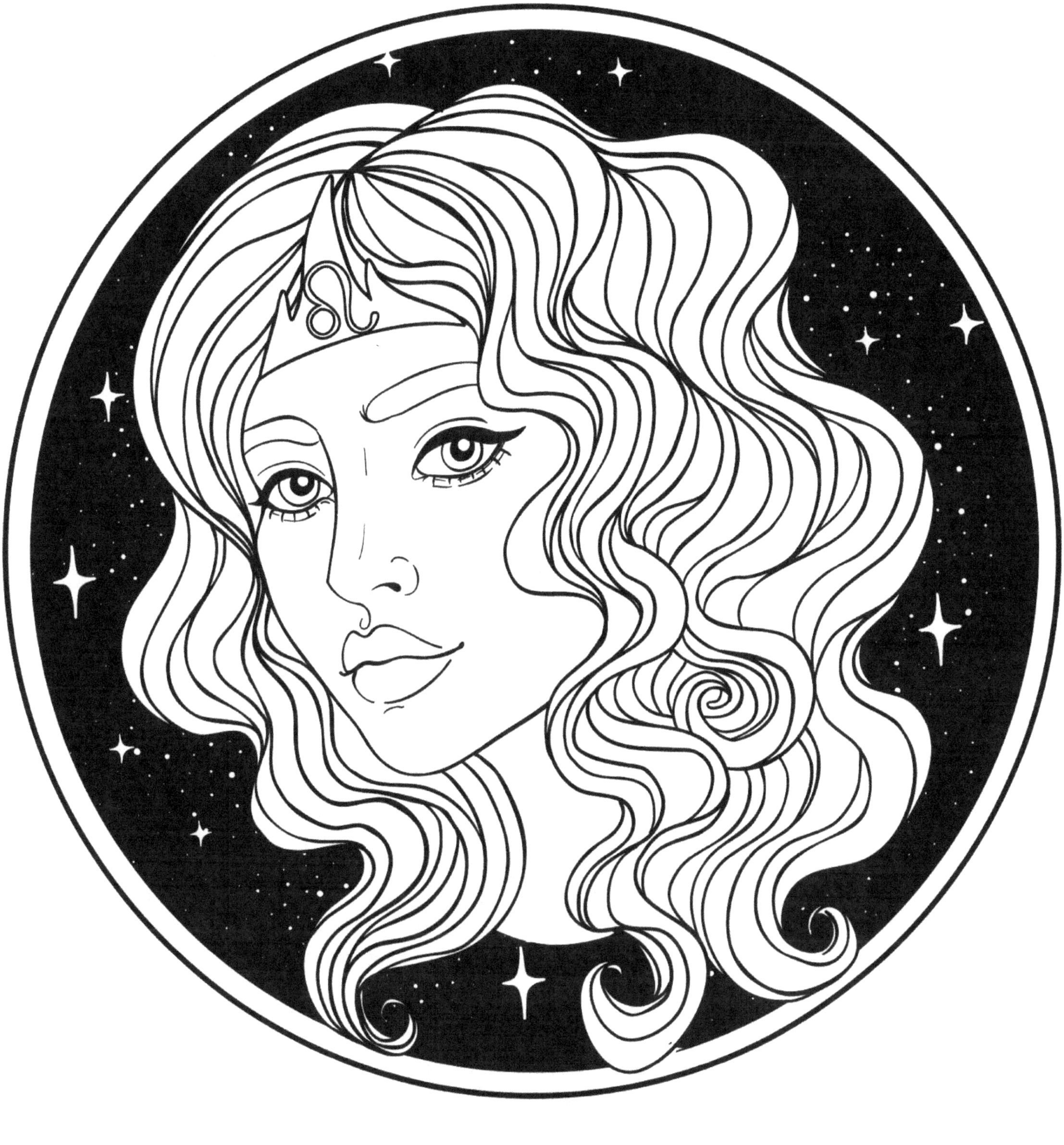

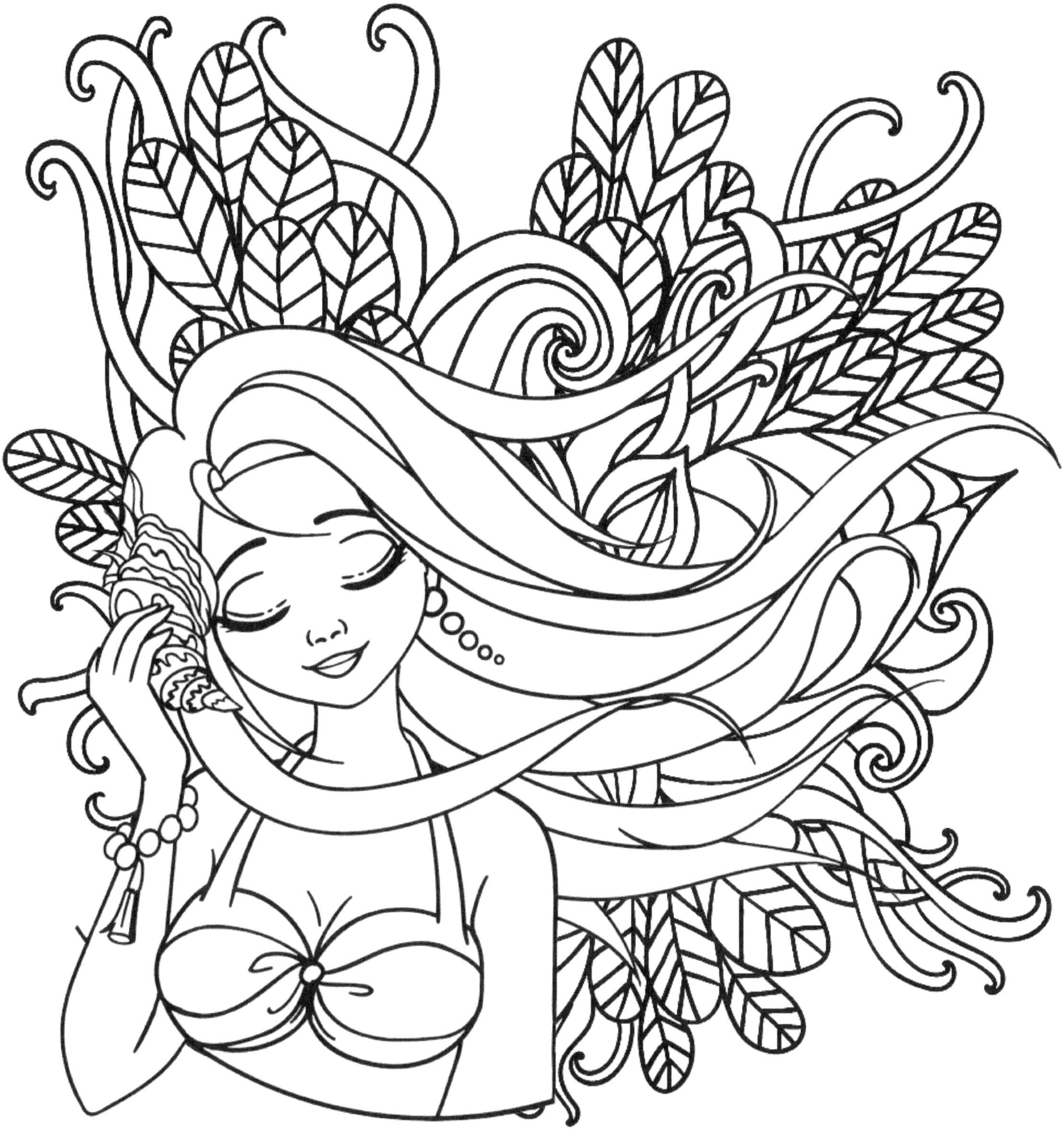

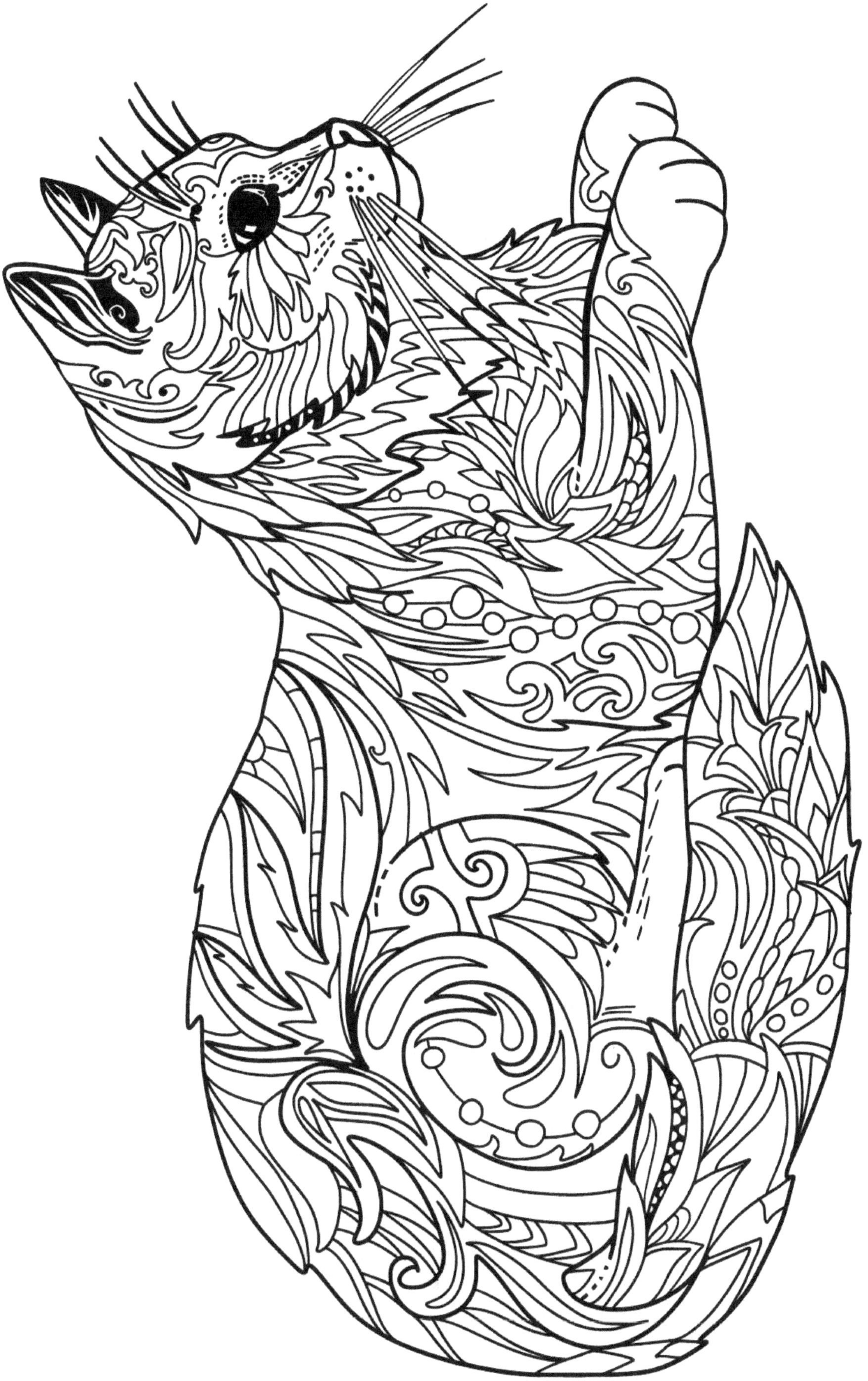

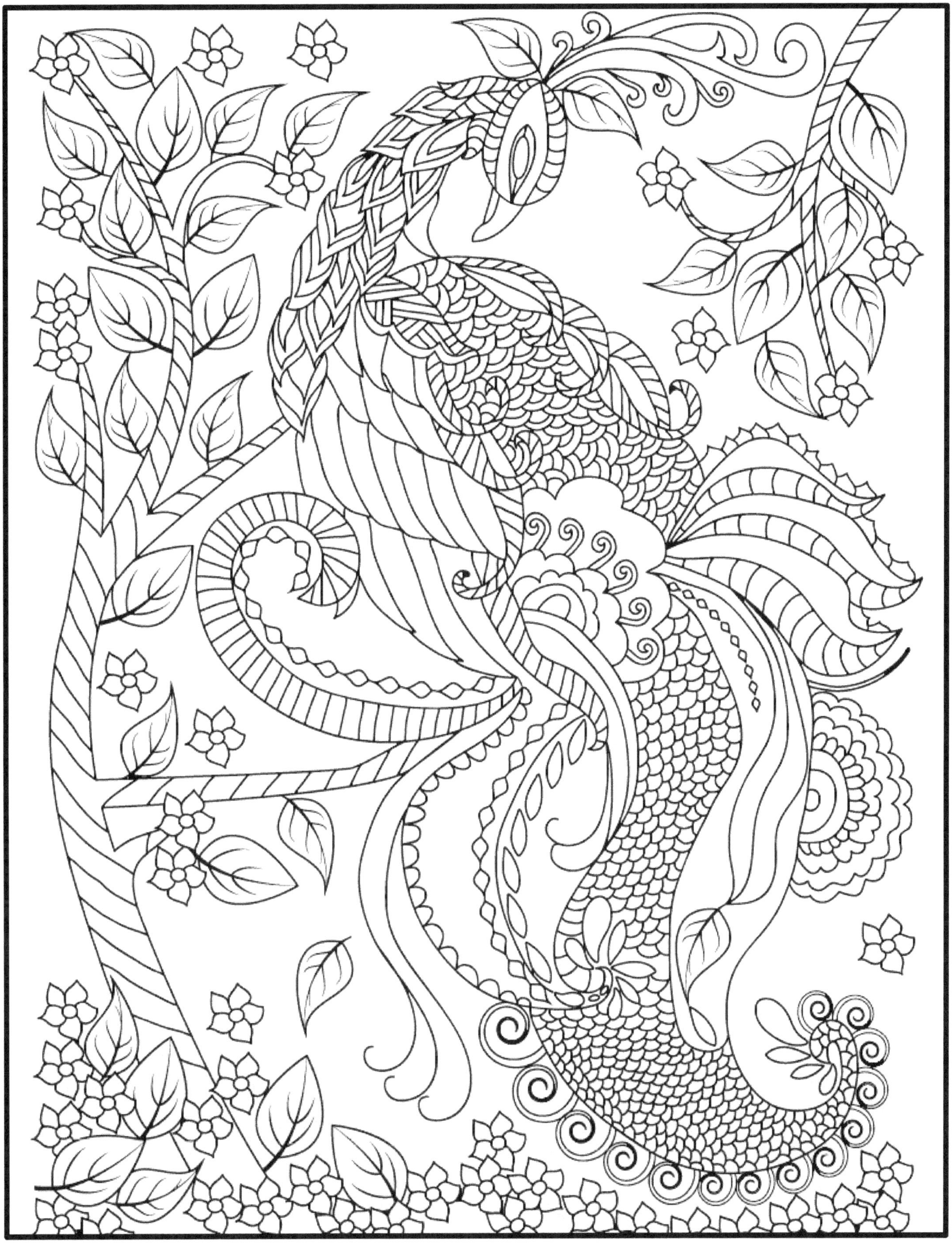

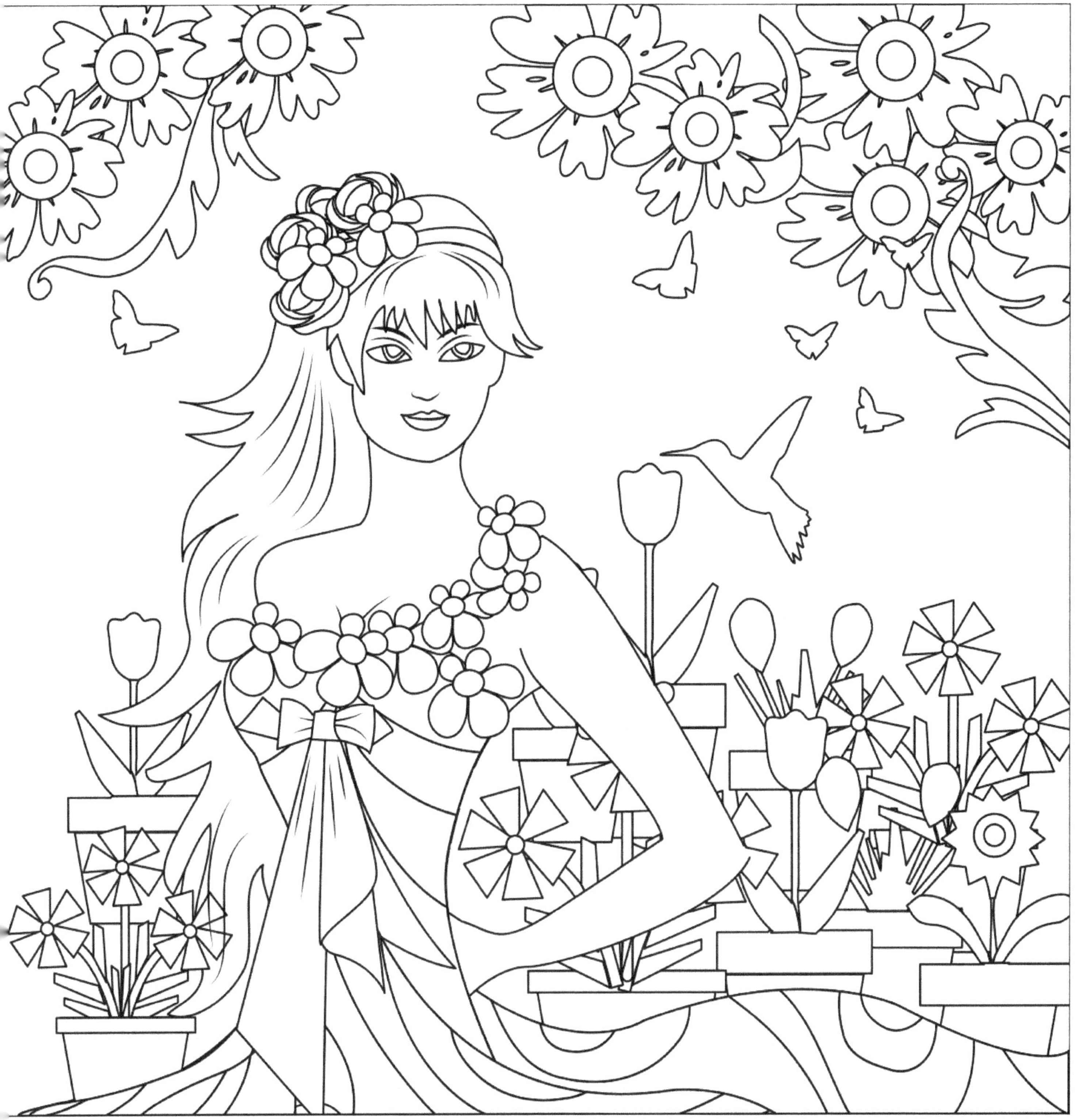

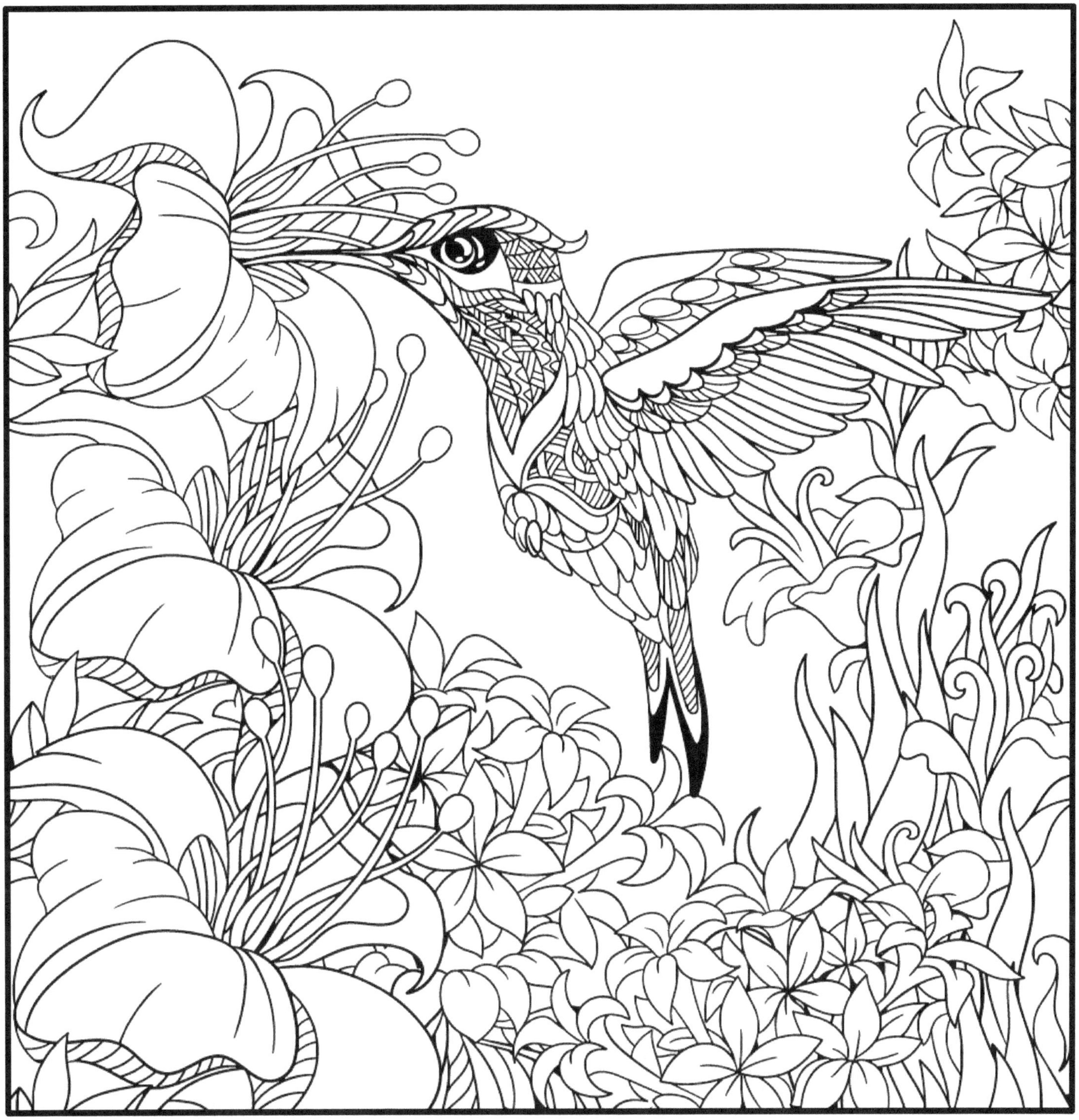

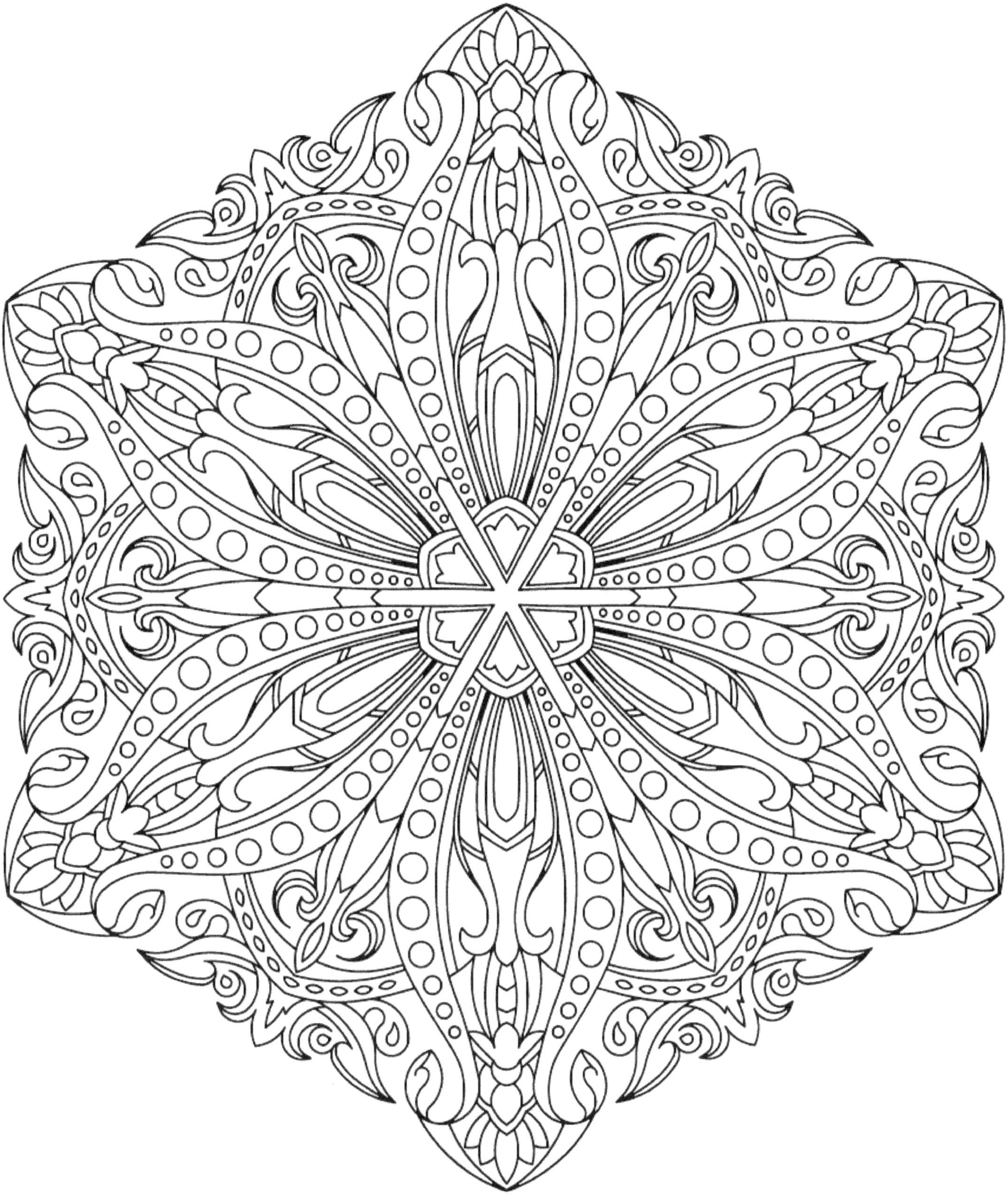

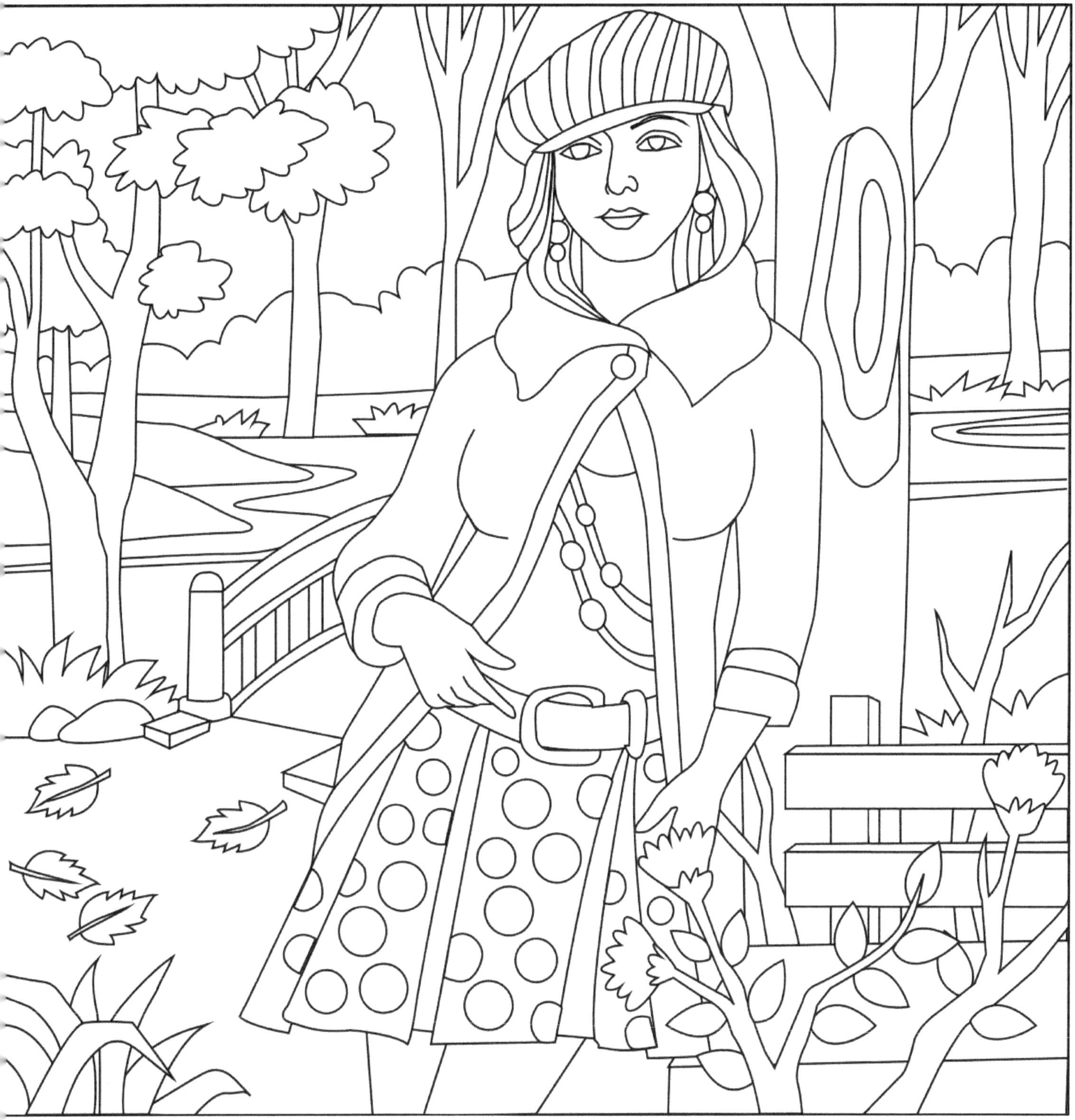

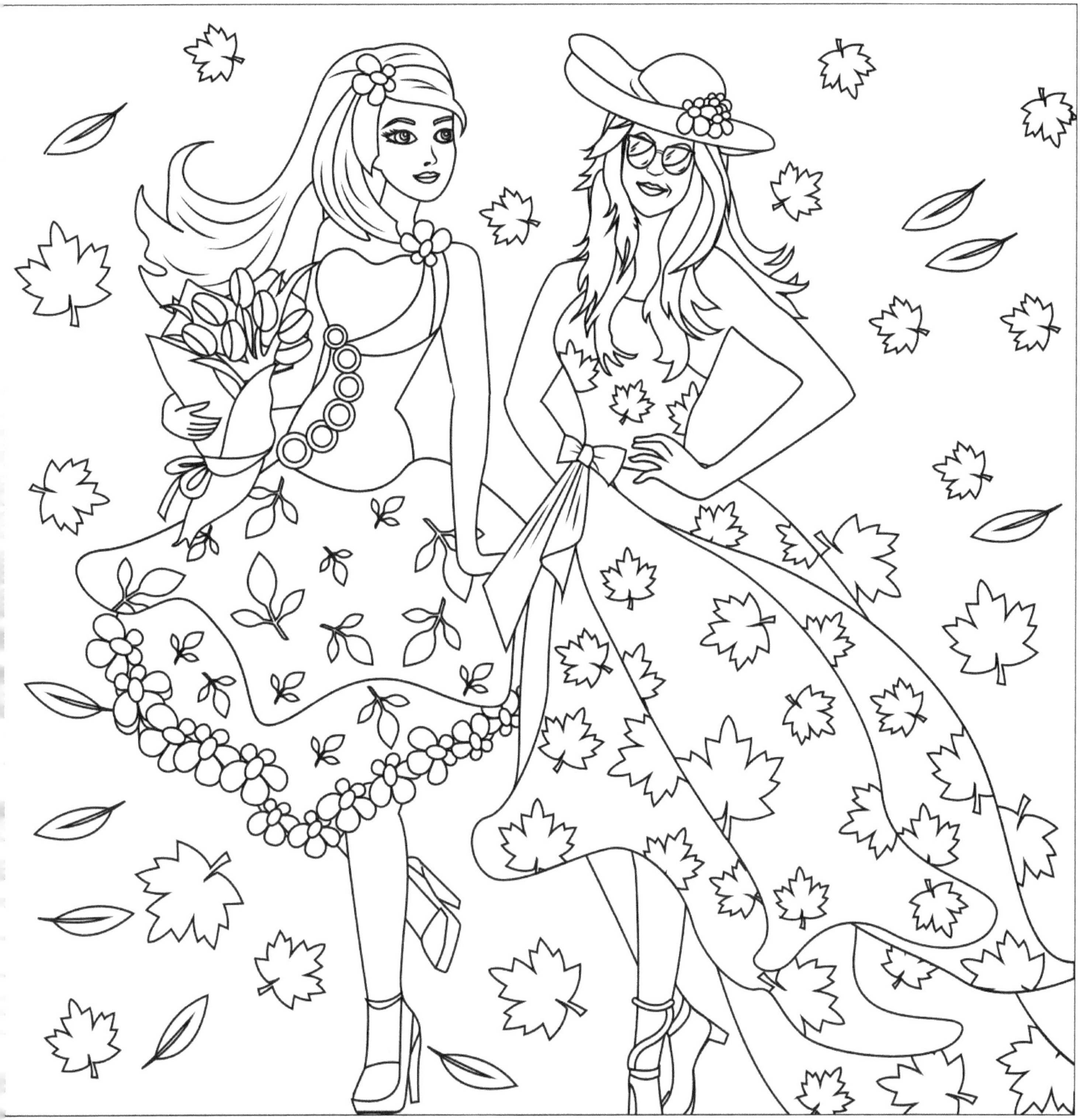

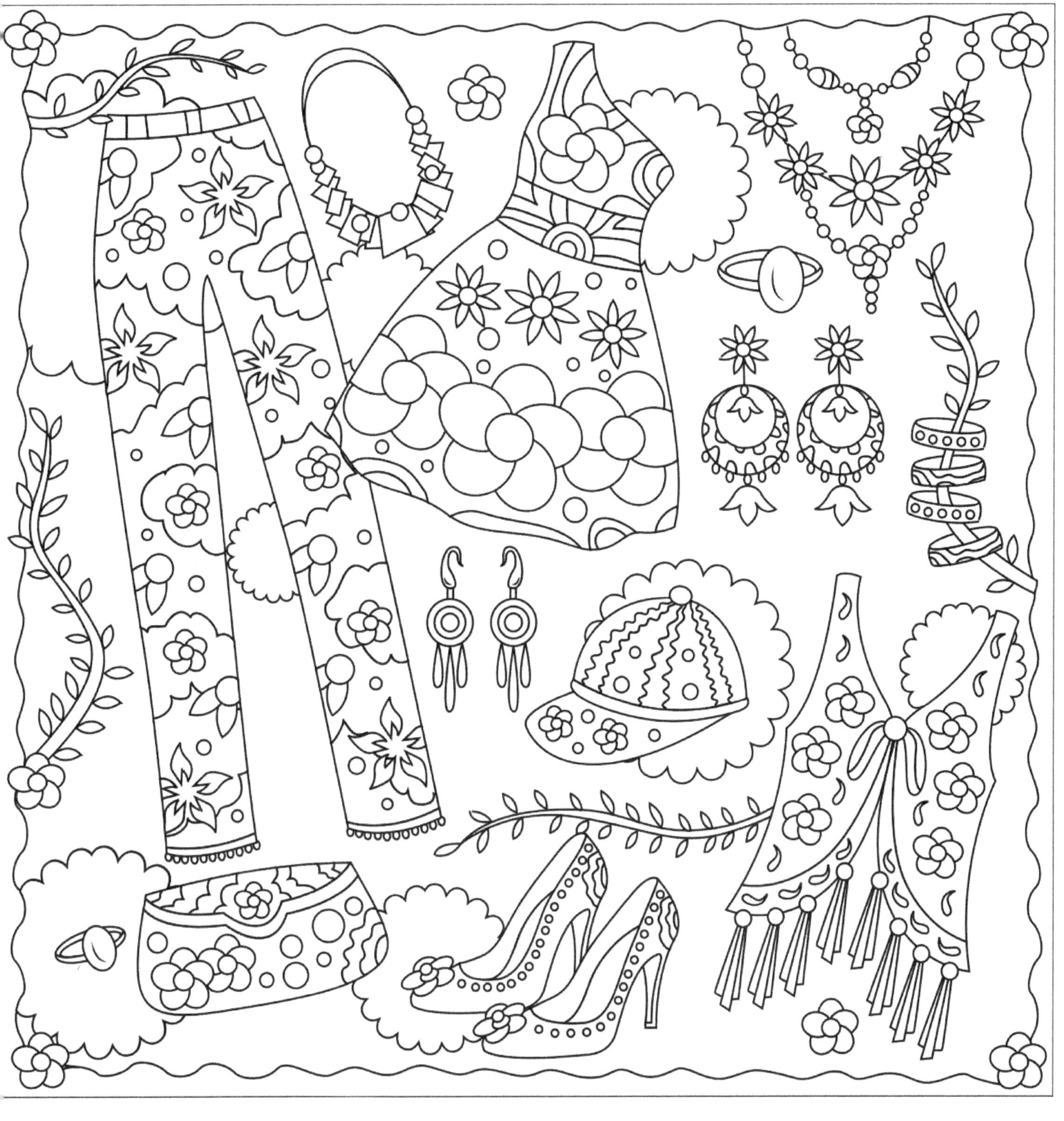

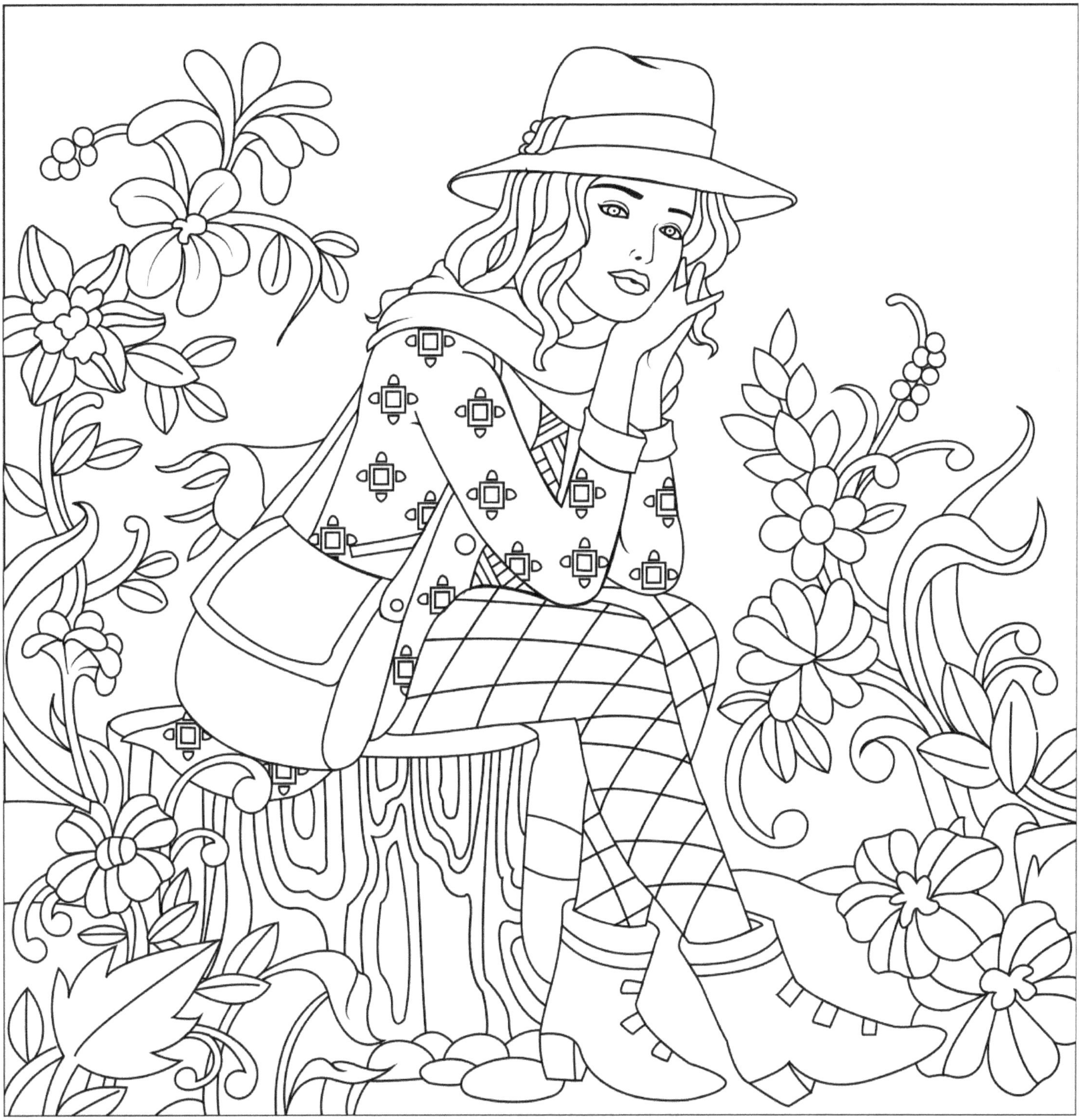

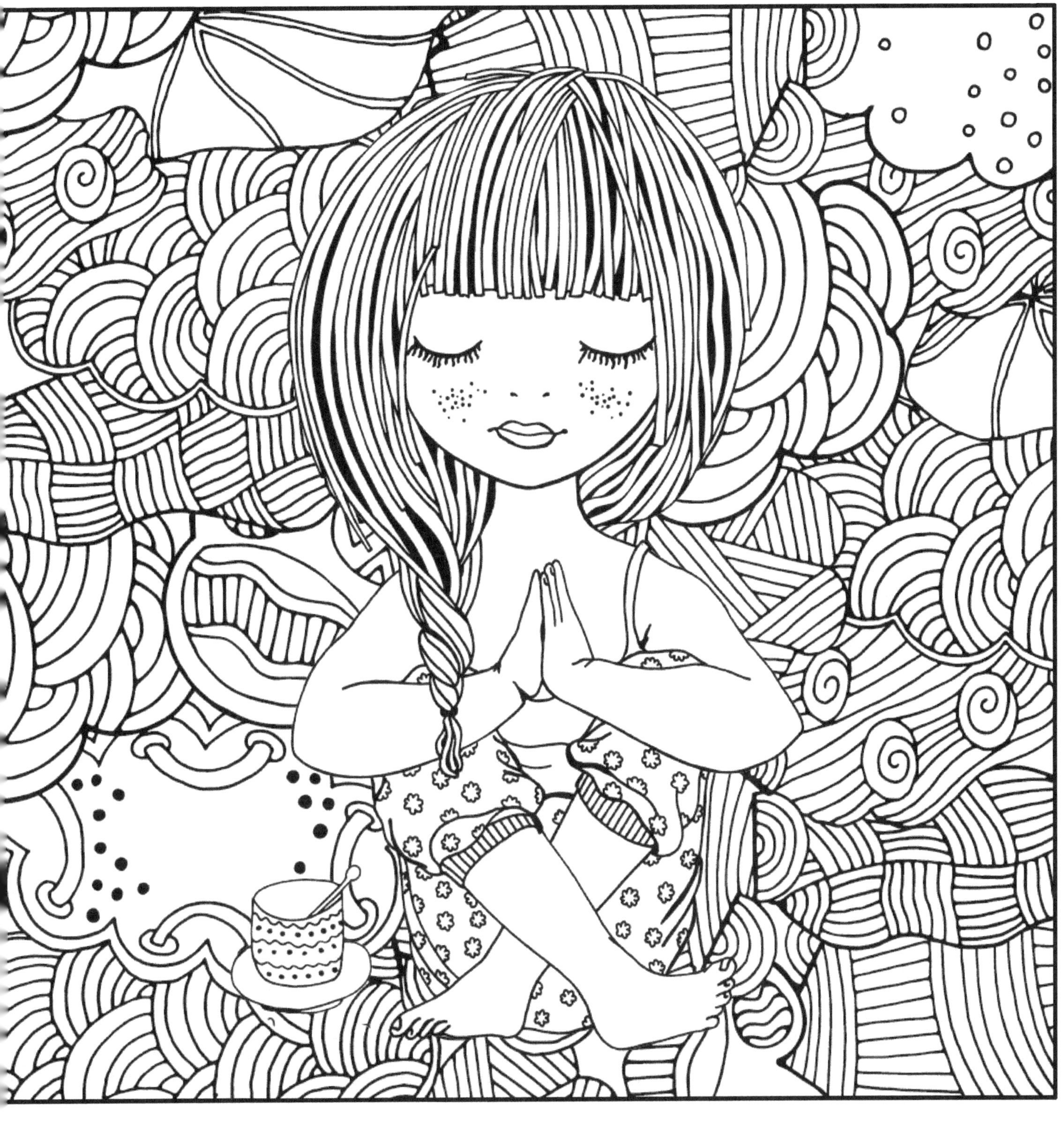

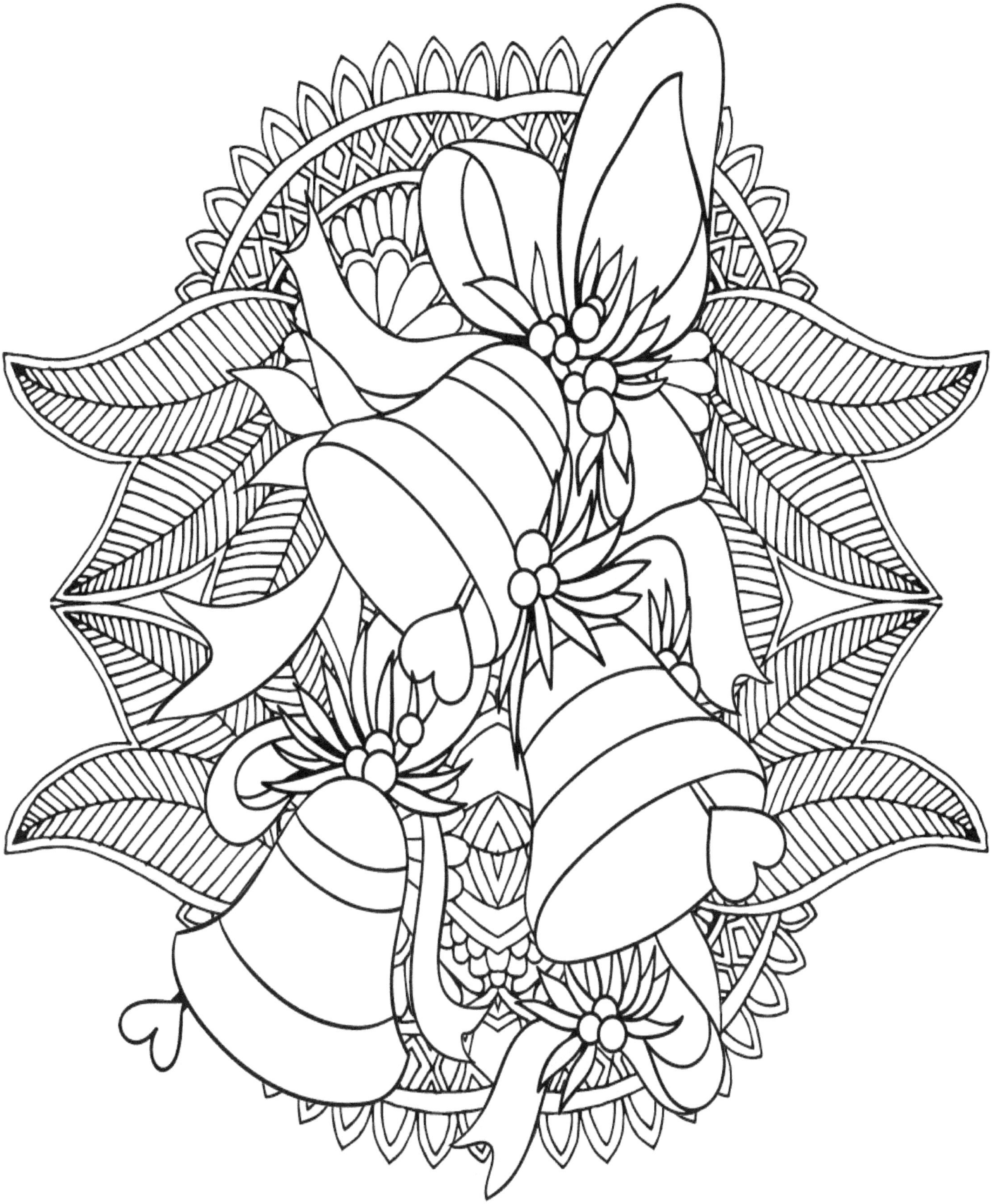

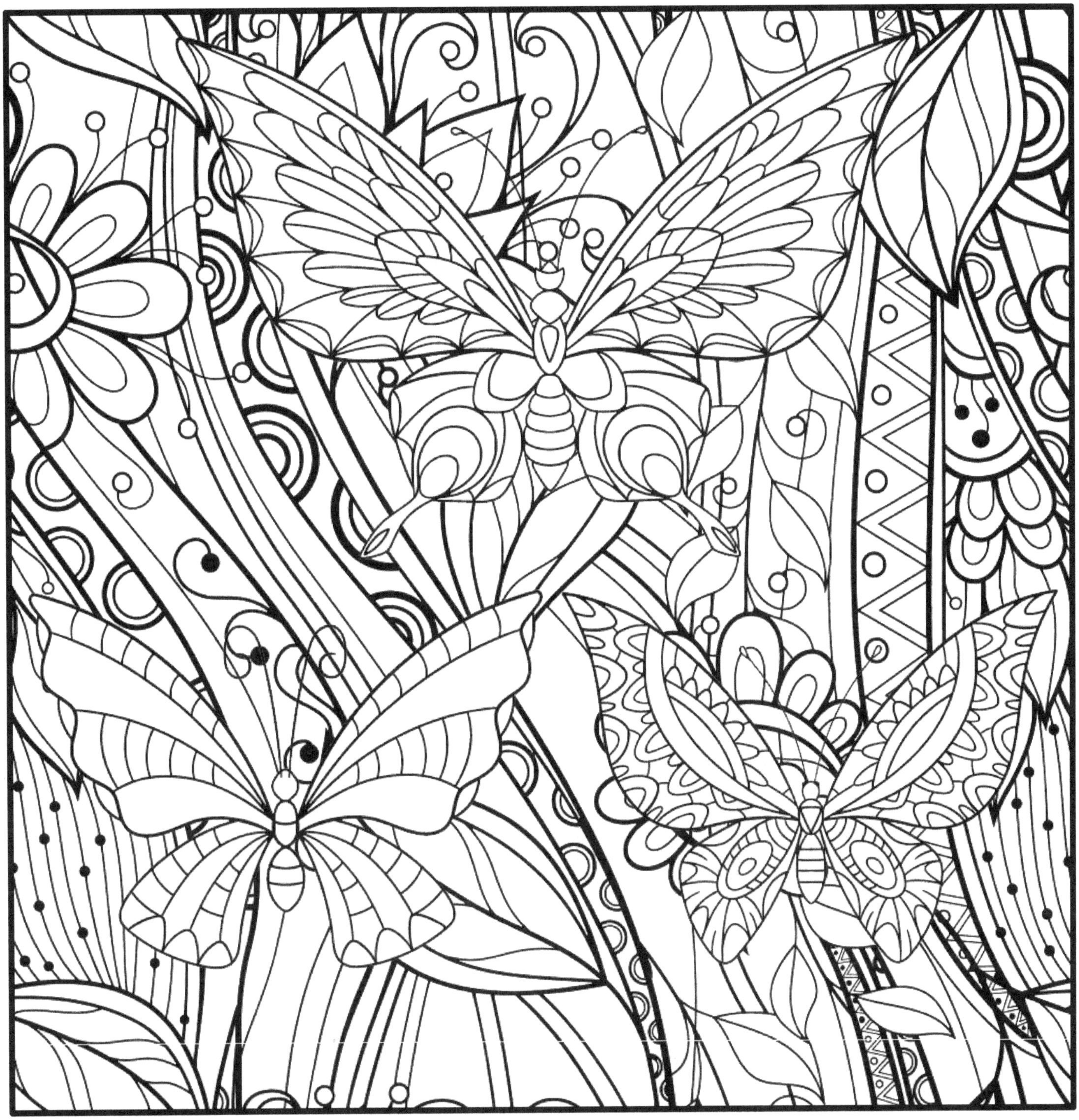

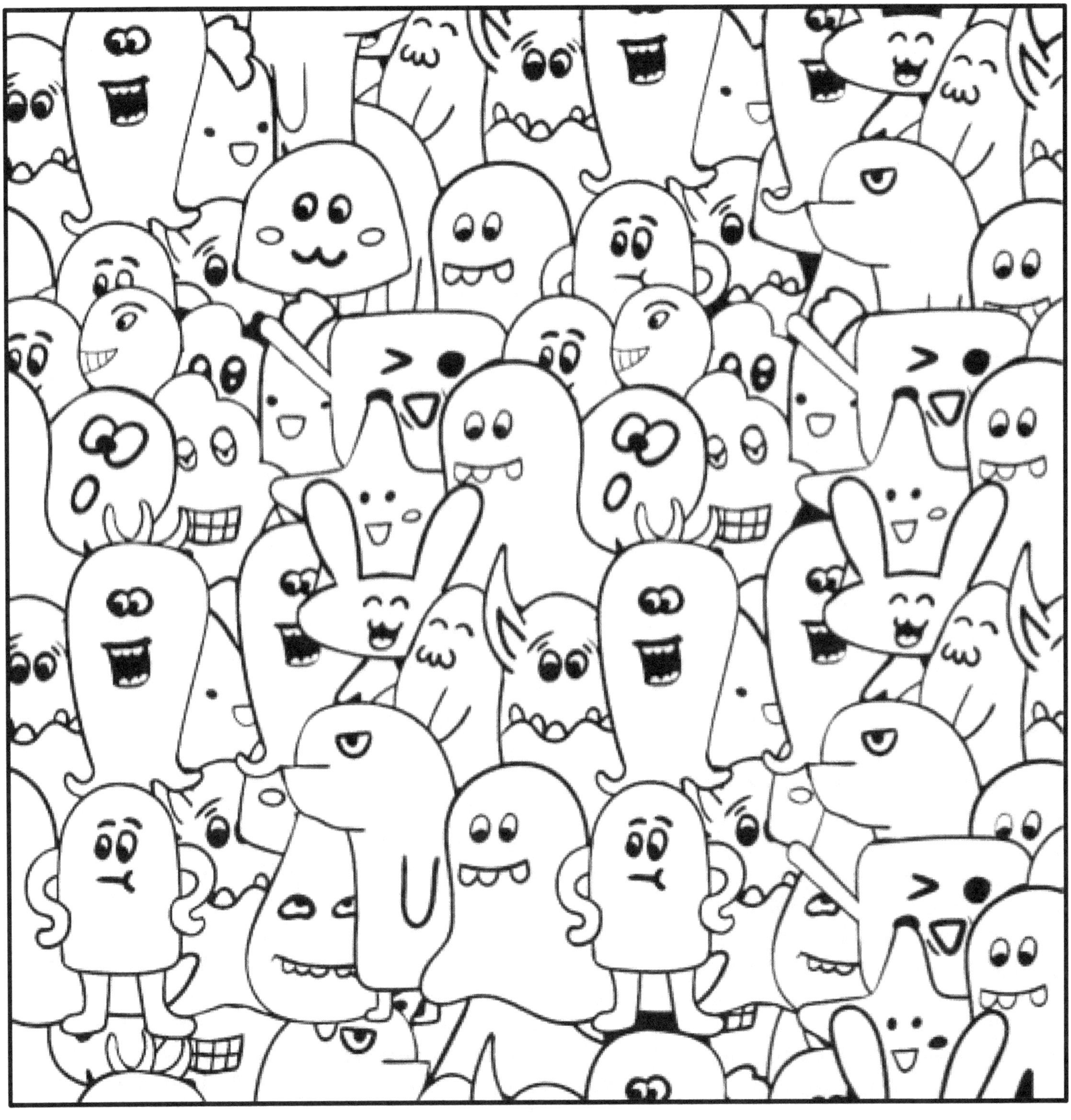

www.ingramcontent.com/pod-product-compliance
Lightning Source LLC
Chambersburg PA
CBHW060434220526
45465CB00008B/3140
9798650407300